D1307009

Endorsements for
The *Handel's Messiah* Family Advent Reader
by Donna W. Payne and Fran Lenzo
Moody Press

"This is an engaging, unique, and inspirational volume for use during the celebration of our Lord's birthday. The text is especially enhanced by the variety of illustrations collected and prepared for this special edition. It will provide fresh and original devotional reading for this sacred time on the Christian calendar."

Dr. D. James Kennedy
President, Coral Ridge Ministries, Television and Radio
Chancellor, Knox Theological Seminary
President, Evangelism Explosion International

"Donna Payne and Fran Lenzo have given all of us a wonderful Christmas present to last all year! Unlike ties and gloves, this gift will never have to be exchanged! Thoroughly enjoyable, spiritually enriching and historically fascinating, 'The Handel's Messiah Family Advent Reader' will be a blessing every Christmas season and at any time of the year!"

Rev. Rob Schenck
General Secretary of The National Clergy Council
Co-founder of The Ten Commandments Project
Author and Evangelist

"Cultural artifacts and traditions serve at least two significant functions in our lives. They offer occasions in which to set our hearts and minds on whatever is true, whatever is noble, whatever is right, whatever is pure, whatever is lovely, whatever is admirable. And they are forms with which we pass on our deepest convictions to our children and our children's children. But many parents are at a loss to know how to share the best cultural forms with their families. Donna Payne and Fran Lenzo have done Christian families a great service by creating a worthy setting for the treasured jewel that is Handel's Messiah. Their Biblical, historical and musical sensitivity will enrich the experience of those who set aside Advent evenings together to prepare for His coming. Their book will deepen the understanding of the providential matrix in which Handel's work has fed so many listeners."

Mr. Ken Myers
Host of Mars Hill Tapes
Former producer for National Public Radio

"What a refreshing book for the entire family to read together four weeks before Christmas. As I read the book, my heart was warmed so that I too responded, '. . . The Lord God omnipotent reigneth!'"

Dr. George Sweeting
Chancellor, Moody Bible Institute
Author and Evangelist

The Handel's Messiah
Family Advent Reader

by

Donna W. Payne

and

Fran Lenzo

MOODY PRESS
CHICAGO

©1999 by DONNA W. PAYNE and FRAN LENZO

All rights reserved. No part of this book may be reproduced in any form without permission in writing from the publisher, except in the case of brief quotations embodied in critical articles or reviews.

The text of Handel's *Messiah* is cited as revised from the King James Version by Charles Jennens. The wordbook used for the text was *Messiah: The Wordbook for the Oratorio* illustrated by Barry Moser with introduction by Christopher Hogwood (New York: Willa Perlman, 1992), which was based on the original 1743 version (first London performance). Text in this book does not always follow capitalization used in the wordbook.

All other Scripture quotations, unless indicated, are taken from the *Holy Bible: New International Version.* "NIV". Copyright © 1973, 1978, 1984 International Bible Society. Used by permission of Zondervan Publishing House. All rights reserved.

The "NIV" and "New International Version" trademarks are registered in the United States Patent and Trademark Office by International Bible Society. Use of either trademark requires permission of International Bible Society.

Scripture quotations marked KJV are taken from the King James Version.

Designed and set by Eagle Publishing, Guildford, Surrey, UK.

ISBN: 0-8024-5574-3

1 3 5 7 9 10 8 6 4 2
Printed in Singapore

George Frideric Handel (1685-1759)
Terra cotta bust by Roubillac (1702-62)

For my husband, Dean,
who knows best
the debt of gratitude I owe him.
And to my dear family
for their loving support.
-D.W.P.

To Bob and Fran Lakin,
for their commitment and love.
To my husband, David, and Rachel, Jo, and Tim,
God's greatest gifts to me.
-F.L.

"Soli Deo Gloria"

Contents

Preface

Contrary to contemporary, popular belief, some things do stand the test of time. In fact, not only do they stand, but they actually become dearer because of surviving the ages. Handel's *Messiah* comes to us from more than two and a half centuries ago, yet the truth of its message and the joy of its music have never stopped inspiring audiences. *Messiah* has been performed somewhere in the world every year since its debut in 1742, according to Richard Luckett, a scholar of Handel's work.

The original score of Messiah, *1742. Coram Foundation, London.*

Messiah initially was intended for Passion Week before Easter, yet now it has become an important part of our annual Christmas tradition. Often only certain portions are performed at that time of year, yet the complete "libretto," the words, of *Messiah* tells the whole story of God's Good News — Christ's birth, death, and resurrection.

Charles Jennens was Handel's librettist, which means he was the one who put together the words of *Messiah*. His skill was evident in how he juxtaposed the Old Testament promises of a Messiah with the New Testament fulfillment of those promises. For this oratorio, Jennens used the 1611 King James Authorized Version as well as the Great Bible of 1539 and the Anglican Book of Common Prayer. Jennens's arrangement is the "wordbook" for Handel's music. He took some liberties in his texts to let the words fit well with the notes and the flow of the music. That is why in some places the verses are slightly different than in the original Bible texts. In this book, we have remained true to Jennens's wording, even keeping his "misspellings," which in reality were the correct spellings of that day. *Messiah* is divided into three parts and includes a preface.

We have chosen to use the "Preface," all the texts from "Part the First," and selected texts from the other two parts. Some of the Scriptures have been grouped together, and some have been split. They remain in the order of their appearance in *Messiah*, except that we have begun and ended with the Revelation passage of the famous "Hallelujah Chorus."

Advent begins the fourth Sunday before Christmas. There are twenty-eight readings altogether, even though the length of Advent varies each year. If the season is shorter than twenty-eight days, please skip to the last reading on Christmas Eve. It was written as a conclusion to Advent and to hail Christ's birth.

We humbly offer this book, as well, to those who are not followers of Christ but who may pick it up because of an interest in Handel's great work. Our interpretations of the libretto are not those of theologians, but of ordinary worshipers in the pew. We believe they represent a classical, historical, ancient understanding of Christian doctrine — perhaps the same understanding that listeners of Handel's time might have had. We hope that in reading these pages readers can better understand the life-giving power of words that are more beautiful to the ears of a needy sinner than any music ever could be.

It was our intention in writing this book to educate as well as to inspire. In our families we have discussed the history of some of our traditions and have reviewed the Christmas story from many different aspects. But year after year questions arise: "Were there really three wise men?" "Why do we stand for the 'Hallelujah Chorus'?" "Did the star actually move to shine above the stable?" It has been a fascinating journey to find out the answers, and we enjoy sharing this information with you. Yet information can remain just "facts."

Spiritual truths can change lives. As parents we have, at times, used stories to illustrate important lessons. Jesus Himself spoke in parables, so that His listeners could better understand what He was teaching them. Here, we have chosen to use that method to explain biblical truths.

We encourage readers going through these stories to read the Scriptures for themselves in their own Bibles and to consider the context of the verses. The cohesiveness and rich meaning of God's truth become clearer as we see His Word in its entirety and not just in small segments.

The accompanying CD of music from *Messiah* should also help prepare your family for Christmas. The end of each entry includes a note about which track(s) on the CD contains the music accompanying that day's text.

This is a book of stories that make us think. May they prompt discussion, conversation, debate, and perhaps some further explanation for younger children. The "Read More About It" section at the end of the book offers some unusual information as well as ideas for expanded study and discovery.

As you prepare for the holidays this year and observe Advent with a sense of anticipation and expectancy, remember the story doesn't end with Christmas. Handel's *Messiah* tells us that Christ's birth is only the beginning. It's not the baby Jesus but rather the crucified and risen Lord Jesus who has the power to change our lives.

"King of kings, and Lord of lords. Hallelujah."

Swords were commonly worn indoors as seen in this 18th century painting

Why the Gentlemen Couldn't Wear Swords

"Hallelujah! For the Lord God Omnipotent reigneth. The kingdom of this world is become the kingdom of our Lord and of His Christ; and He shall reign for ever and ever, King of Kings, and Lord of Lords. Hallelujah!"
— based on Revelation 19:6; 11:15; 19:16

The advertisement had this warning for people who planned on going to the concert: Ladies should not "come with hoops," and "Gentlemen are desired to come without their swords." This notice appeared more than 250 years ago when men wore forty-inch swords for dressy occasions and fashionable ladies put giant hoops in the bottoms of their gold- and silver-trimmed skirts.

The notice was published because the hit composer George Frideric Handel was going to present his new masterpiece, *Messiah*, for the first time. So many people were expected to attend the concert that organizers didn't think there would be enough room unless the concert goers left their swords and hoops at home.

Sure enough, that first concert was successful. The local newspaper reported that Handel's *Messiah* was "allowed by the greatest Judges to be the finest Composition of Musick that was ever heard." Lots of people today would agree with those old-time reporters. Then as now, Handel was known around the world.

He was born in Germany, worked in Italy writing operas, and finally settled in England as a favorite composer of King George I. That first performance of *Messiah* was in Dublin, Ireland. He wrote it as a fund-raiser for three charities (two hospitals and a jail). After he received the invitation to present a concert for charity in Dublin, Handel set to work writing *Messiah*. He wrote it at an amazing pace, taking just twenty-four days total, from August 22 to September 14 of 1741.

Messiah was performed many times during Handel's lifetime, often with him directing or playing an instrument. Almost always, the concerts were given to raise money for orphans or hospitals or other needy causes. From the beginning, *Messiah* was Handel's gift to the world. There are lots of stories about how he wrote *Messiah*. People say that he barely ate or drank or slept. We hear that his servant would bring him hot chocolate in the morning and find him crying as he worked. Others say that his papers were marked with his tears. But we will never know what Handel was really thinking or feeling when he wrote *Messiah*, because he did not leave any letters or notes to tell us. We do know that many who have heard his beautiful words and music have cried as they listened.

While Handel was alive, one man wrote his friend, "I would ride forty miles in the wind and rain to be present at a performance of the *Messiah*." Handel is said to have told a nobleman friend the reason he wrote *Messiah:* "I should be sorry," Handel remarked, "if I only entertained them. I wished to make them better."

Messiah is an oratorio — music that tells a Bible message using a choir and orchestra. *Messiah* is the most popular oratorio ever written. It has been sung (especially at Christmastime) by good singers and bad singers, by choruses of twenty-five people and choruses of more than a thousand people. London, Chicago, and New York have celebrated with *Messiah* concerts performed by thousands of singers and hundreds of instruments.

Bigger is not necessarily better. Handel performed his oratorio with different types of singers and instruments, but the group was always small in size. He might have had a few boy singers, several soloists, and ten or so adults in the chorus.

Since Handel's time, *Messiah* has been performed so often and in so many different ways that some music experts have become bored with it. But for those who listen, *Messiah* has a wonderful story to tell. *Messiah* tells the story of Jesus. It is the story of His coming (Advent), of His birth (the Christmas story), and of His death and resurrection (the Easter story).

The words of *Messiah* are from the Bible but were chosen and arranged by Handel's friend, Charles Jennens. All the verses together are called the "libretto." Each of the Advent readings in this book will tell a story related to one of the sets of Bible verses from *Messiah*. Today's selection is the most famous. It presents the words of the "Hallelujah Chorus." (You will be able to find out more about the "Hallelujah Chorus" in the story for Christmas Eve.)

Hallelujah is a Hebrew word that means "Praise the Lord." It is a good word for the beginning of Advent. We can shout Hallelujah for the baby Jesus who is really the "King of kings" and the omnipotent (all-powerful) God who came to earth to bring each one of us the incredible gift of salvation.

This entry is accompanied by track 26 on the CD.

Secret of the Desert Caves

"And without controversy, great is the mystery of godli-
ness: God was manifested in the flesh, justified by the
Spirit, seen of angels, preached among the Gentiles,
believed on in the world, received up in glory."
— based on 1 Timothy 3:16

Muhammed el-Hamed, called "edh-Dhib" (the Wolf), a bedouin shepherd of the Taamireh tribe, discovered a great treasure of books in
a desert cave beyond Bethlehem. They are books of mystery, books
that had been hidden for a long time. They speak of a Messiah and Savior. Who
wrote these books and why? What do they all say and mean?

The most common version of the discovery of the books goes like this.
Sometime in the year 1947, edh-Dhib was tending his goats in the mountain-
ous desert near the uppermost tip of the Dead Sea, not far from Bethlehem and
Jerusalem. One of his animals wandered off and was lost. Edh-Dhib scrambled
up a steep, dry mountainside to search for it and came upon a hole, one of the
many caves in that area. The shepherd, thinking he heard his goat hiding in the
cave, threw a rock inside, hoping to scare the animal out. But instead of the
sound of rock hitting rock, edh-Dhib heard the sound of something breaking.

Later, he returned to the cave with his friends. There they found large pot-
tery jars containing seven old, blackened, smelly rolls of leather. The shepherds
recognized that these old things might have some value and took them to
Bethlehem to sell. That first cave and others discovered later contained a treasure of ancient books. They were scrolls — books written on rolled-up lengths
of leather, papyrus (reed paper), and, in one case, copper. Eventually, nearly
three hundred caves were explored in the Dead Sea area. Eleven contained
scrolls or pieces of scrolls.

The seven scrolls from the first cave ended up in the hands of a group of religious leaders and scholars. One of the first American archaeologists to see
copies of the scrolls called them an "incredible find." And so they were. The
copper scroll found in cave 3 is a list of treasure buried around the Dead Sea
area. The treasure would be worth millions of dollars if anyone could find it.
The other scrolls are copies of books from the times before and after the birth
of Jesus.

The Dead Sea Scrolls include parts or the whole of every book in the Old
Testament except Esther. The scrolls are one thousand years older than any

copies of the Bible found before them, yet they are nearly identical to the Old Testament books we have today. They show that, throughout the ages, the scribes who copied God's book have done so with an incredible accuracy that helps us to have faith in the truthfulness of the words we read today.

Most of the scrolls were found in the caves visible on this rocky outcrop near Qumran

Near the caves are the ancient ruins of Qumran, the remains of a Jewish religious community from around the time of Christ's birth. Most scholars believe that these were the people who kept the books. Some of the scrolls tell about this group. Like most Jews of that time, the people of the Qumran community were waiting for a Messiah, a Savior of Israel. Some of their writings describe their ideas about the Messiah.

For centuries, people like those at Qumran and all over Israel hoped for a Messiah. The Old Testament parts of their scrolls told them something about the promised Messiah. He would be born in Bethlehem of King David's line and would bring peace and righteousness to the world. But no one knew when the Messiah would come or what exactly He would do. Christians believe that the mystery was solved with the birth of a Jewish baby two thousand years ago.

The long-awaited Messiah and Savior is Jesus, born in Bethlehem of King David's family line. The New Testament says that Jesus is "the mystery that has been kept hidden for ages" (Colossians 1:25–27) and is now shown to us.

Every year, during the few weeks before Christmas, Christians remember the long wait for the Messiah. That is what the Advent season is all about. Advent means "coming." As Christians wait with excitement for the coming of Christmas, they are acting a little like the people who waited for the coming of the Messiah. In our time, that waiting is over and the mystery has been revealed. Now instead, we wait for the time when Jesus will come again in glory to judge the world and bring everlasting peace.

Just as the secrets of the desert caves were finally discovered after so many years, so the mystery of the Messiah was finally revealed in Jesus. The description of Jesus in today's Bible verse is a wonderful summary of who He is. That is why these are the first words that appear in Handel's musical story of the Messiah, though they are part of the preface that is never sung.

God became human. Jesus was proven to be God by His miracles. Angels announced His coming and served Him. Jews and Gentiles believed He was God. He returned to heaven, and one day He will come again to make all things right.

Finding the Perfect Gift

*"In whom [Christ] are hid all the treasures of wisdom
and knowledge."*
— based on Colossians 2:3

Gifts, presents, treasures. Get them or give them. Want them, wait for them, wonder about them, or worry about them. Gifts seem to be what Christmas is all about.

At the beginning of this century, William Sydney Porter wrote a story about Christmas presents. He called it "The Gift of the Magi." Just as he did for all his stories, he wrote it using the name of "O. Henry." "The Gift of the Magi" is one of the most popular of all Christmas stories, and it begins this way: "One dollar and eighty-seven cents. That was all. And sixty cents of it was in pennies."

O. Henry's story is about Della, the woman who had the one dollar and eighty-seven cents. It was all of her Christmas money, all she had been able to save to buy a present for her husband, Jim. Jim's salary was twenty dollars a week. Even in those days, that wasn't enough to have extra for gifts. Della had saved her pennies one by one out of the grocery money. When Christmas Eve came, with only one dollar and eighty-seven cents put aside to buy something for Jim, she wanted to cry. She couldn't buy something wonderful with just those few coins.

Then Della remembered her treasure. It was one of the two treasures in that poor little family. Della's was her long, brown, beautiful hair. Jim's treasure was a gold watch that had come down to him from his father and grandfather.

O. Henry wrote that Della and Jim were so proud of Jim's watch that they were sure that it was better than any of King Solomon's riches. And they loved her hair so much that they felt like the Queen of Sheba would have been jealous of it.

But because Della loved Jim more than she loved her hair, she sold it to a lady who made fancy wigs. Della got twenty dollars for her hair, enough to buy the perfect gift for Jim — a long, lovely silver-white chain to hold and show off his precious watch. Jim, too, had found the perfect gift for Della. O. Henry's story ends with Jim giving Della her Christmas present — a set of jeweled combs to hold up her long hair. Della had admired the combs in a shop window, but she didn't expect to own them someday. They were such expensive combs that Jim had needed to sell his watch to buy them for Della.

The three wise men bring gifts to the baby Jesus in this oil by Rembrandt

So Della had her hair ornaments but not the hair to put them in, and Jim had a lovely chain, but no watch to hang on it. Della and Jim, wrote O. Henry, were "two foolish children . . . who most unwisely sacrificed for each other the greatest treasures of their house." But, he continued, "of all who give gifts these two were the wisest."

At Christmastime we hear a lot about gifts of love and about using our hearts and our treasures wisely in order to find the right Christmas spirit. Perhaps that is why O. Henry's story is so popular. We admire Della's and Jim's sacrifices. We know that the love they had for each other was more valuable than the expensive Christmas presents that they had bought. We realize that presents can get old and boring, clothes wear out, and gadgets break, but love is the gift that really satisfies. Almost everyone wants to experience such peace and love at Christmas.

But sometimes there is a difference between what we know and what we feel. We would like to have Della and Jim's wise Christmas spirit, but sometimes it just doesn't seem possible. Relatives or friends might drive us crazy. There are times when we don't feel loving or lovable. There are times of sadness, even at Christmas. At times like these, the talk about the true meaning of Christmas seems a little bit unrealistic. At such times, the presents gleaming bright and beautiful for us under the Christmas tree seem more attractive than the troublesome people or events that come our way.

At Christmas and all year round, we need more than good intentions and happy thoughts. We need God's help. We need God's presence. We need wisdom to live rightly and to love rightly. The beginning of the Bible's book of Proverbs tells us that God's wisdom brings life, joy, peace, safety, justice, righteousness, and faithfulness. His wisdom is the gift we all need, the gift we all want. It is the most perfect of Christmas gifts.

In Christ we find the wisdom that we long for. His treasures alone bring real meaning to our Christmases and to our lives.

Christmas Truce

*"Comfort ye, comfort ye my people, saith your God;
speak ye comfortably to Jerusalem, and cry unto her,
that her warfare is accomplished, that her iniquity is
pardon'd."*

— based on Isaiah 40:1–2

When Christmas came in 1914, in the first year of World War I, the soldiers were in their trenches on the battlefront, weary from the sights and sounds of warfare. For hundreds of miles along the battle line, both sides had dug rows of ditches and underground supply rooms. Each side's trenches faced the other, separated only by barbed wire and a narrow strip of "no-man's-land." A trench soldier shared his sleeping bag with rats and bugs and frogs.

Sometimes he was knee-deep in mud and water. At Christmastime the soldiers had freezing rain and snow and ice. Always, there was either the memory or the reality of rifle fire, of the earsplitting explosions of big guns and rockets, of the rat-a-tat-tat of machine gun fire and the brilliant light of exploding shells in the night sky. How could there be Christmas peace in a place like that?

Back home, wives, mothers, fathers, sons, and daughters waited for their soldiers, hoping for a peace that did not come for four more years. That Christmas, the shops did a record business, post offices were overworked, and trains were busy with the business of sending Christmas packages to the trenches. People sent hand-knit clothes, sweet cakes, gloves, photographs, and letters.

The French military organized deliveries of holiday gifts for their soldiers and bought all the plum puddings they could find to send to British soldiers. In England, newspapers and clubs raised money to send presents to the troops. Hotels printed war pictures on their menus. King George and Queen Mary sent a Christmas card to each British soldier. The French government delivered Christmas gifts from Germany to their German prisoners of war. *The New York Times* reporter in Paris wrote, "The spirit of those at home is not to give presents to one another, but to unite and give all to the son, father, or brother serving with the flag."

That outpouring of gifts and love was an effort to bring a few moments of comfort and peace to young men at war. The Christmas prayers and concern of the families at home were not unusual for nations at war. But that Christmas of

1914, here and there along the trenches, something unusual did happen.

Without official approval, sometimes against orders, and almost by accident, the soldiers in the trenches made for themselves a Christmas truce. Up and down the line, at different times and in different places, the guns were silent. A few soldiers called out, or sang, or even stood up and approached the other side. "We don't want to kill you. Don't shoot," they would shout. In some places, German and British soldiers sang Christmas carols together, each in his own language. In others, they met in the middle of no-man's-land and exchanged chocolate, tins of jam, cigarettes, souvenirs, and addresses. They shook hands and showed photographs of their families. In one place, Irish soldiers lined up with their German enemies to take a photograph together. In another, German and Scottish soldiers laid down their hats for goalposts and played a game of soccer.

In some places the Christmas truce lasted only hours. In others, it lasted for several days. But everywhere it ended. In the north of France, big guns from boats at sea began firing at the end of Christmas Day "in a blazing fireworks display." German and British officers climbed to the tops of their trenches, saluted each other, and fired shots into the air, signaling that the war had started again.

World War I, "The Great War," ended in 1918. It was supposed to be "the war to end all wars." But, of course, it was not. Since that time, there have been big and little wars between nations. The world even saw a second "world war." Many countries still have hatreds between peoples of different races and religions. Anger causes problems between friends. Families have arguments. A war between good and evil is fought in each person's soul.

We are at war with each other, with ourselves, and, most of all, with God. The prophet Isaiah tells us to be comforted. Our sins can be forgiven and our warfare ended. A peace treaty between God and man was accomplished by the God-man, Jesus, when He paid the penalty for the sins of the world on a cross.

Be comforted. One day there will be peace on earth. Now and forever, we can have peace for our souls. Jesus came to Bethlehem to provide a Christmas truce that never ends.

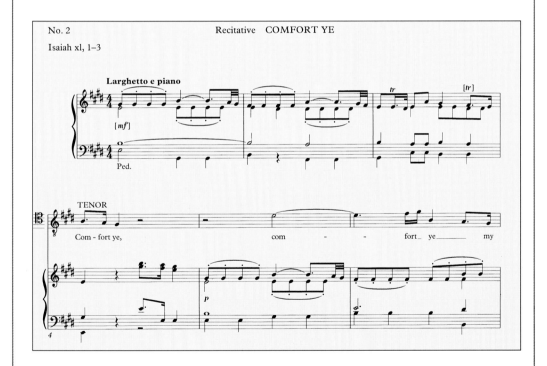

This entry is accompanied by track 1 on the CD.

The Messenger

"The voice of him that crieth in the wilderness, Prepare
ye the way of the Lord, make straight in the desert a
highway for our God. Every valley shall be exalted, and
every mountain and hill made low, the crooked straight,
and the rough places plain."
— based on Isaiah 40:3-4

From Elijah to Malachi to Zechariah to Elizabeth to John to Jesus this is a story of Advent, of waiting and of getting ready. Once there was a man of God by the name of Elijah. He lived long ago and was a prophet, one who speaks the word of the Lord. Elijah lived in the wilderness and wore a coat of sheep or goat hair with a leather belt around his waist. He warned people to repent of their sins and turn back to God. When the time of his ministry was over, God took him to heaven in a whirlwind accompanied by horses and chariots of fire.

Later God made a promise about Elijah through another prophet whose name was Malachi. This was God's promise, written in Malachi's book, the last book of the Old Testament: "I will send my messenger, who will prepare the way before me" (Malachi 3:1). Later He said, "I will send you the prophet Elijah. . . . He will turn the hearts of the fathers to their children, and the hearts of the children to their fathers" (4:5-6).

Malachi was not the only prophet to tell of a messenger. Isaiah also spoke about one who would "prepare the way for the Lord" (Isaiah 40:3). These promises were written hundreds of years before Jesus, the Savior and Messiah, was born. For all that time, people waited and watched for the messenger Elijah to come help them get ready for the Savior. Finally, the waiting ended and the first sign of a messenger came to Zechariah, an old man who belonged to one of the priestly families in Israel.

Each of these families took turns, one week at a time, serving in the temple at Jerusalem. During the week of Zechariah's service, he was chosen by lot to burn incense in the temple. This sweet-smelling offering to God was made twice each day and signified the prayers of God's people. A priest such as Zechariah typically had this honor only once in his lifetime.

As Zechariah made the offering, he was alone in the Holy Place, with people praying outside. The angel Gabriel appeared to him at the right side of the altar of incense. The angel's message was astounding. Zechariah and his wife,

Elizabeth, would have a baby, and they were to name the child John. Their son would be a delight to them and would be "great in the sight of the Lord." This John, the angel said, would "go on before the Lord, in the spirit and power of Elijah, to turn the hearts of the fathers to their children . . . to make ready a people prepared for the Lord" (Luke 1:17).

Zechariah knew the ancient promise that a messenger would come to prepare the way for the Savior. But he and his wife had never had any children and they were, by then, too old to have babies. Zechariah could not believe that Elizabeth would give birth to any son, let alone such a son as the angel spoke of. So Gabriel gave another sign. Because Zechariah did not believe God, he would not be able to speak until the child was born. Then he would see with his own eyes that the promise had come true.

Zechariah and Elizabeth did have a son, and when Zechariah wrote that his child was named John, he was able to speak once more. Zechariah began by praising God and saying this about his son, "You, my child, will . . . prepare the way for [the Lord], to give his people the knowledge of salvation through the forgiveness of their sins" (Luke 1:76-77).

The traditional site of baptism in the River Jordan, from a 19th century drawing

When John grew up, he lived in the desert. He wore a coat of camel's hair and had a leather belt around his waist. He was called John the Baptist because he baptized people in the river. People came from all around the region to hear him preach. His message was a prophet's message, the message of Elijah. He told his listeners to repent of their sins.

When Jesus spoke to His disciples about John, He told them that John was the promised messenger and "the Elijah who was to come" (Matthew 11:14) Later, all of the gospel writers also reported that John was the messenger that Isaiah and Malachi had written about. John was not Elijah come to life again. Rather, he was the last of the prophets who came before Christ, the last messenger to warn people to get ready. John preached, as the angel Gabriel had announced, in the spirit and power of Elijah.

The message of Elijah, Isaiah, Malachi, John, and all of the prophets was an Advent message, a getting-ready message. They preached that whoever would welcome the Savior into their lives must first "prepare the way" by repentance. Our ways are crooked and rough, and our hearts are lonely like a desert. It is only when we admit that we are sinners and turn away from our sin that we are ready to receive the forgiveness of the Savior. Then the Advent waiting is over and Christmas arrives.

Part of the text of this entry is accompanied by track 2 on the CD.

Star of Wonder

*"And the glory of the Lord shall be revealed, and all flesh
shall see it together; for the mouth of the Lord hath
spoken it."*

— based on Isaiah 40:5

Stars are made of many materials: tinfoil stars, paper stars, jewelry stars, plastic stars, musical stars, battery-operated stars, and kid-colored crayon stars. In modern times, the appearance of Christmas stars marks the beginning of a wild buying season. Two thousand years ago, the Christmas star led wise men to look for Jesus.

The story of the Bethlehem star is told only in the gospel of Matthew (chapter 2, verses 1–12). In that record there are lots of clues about the star and its meaning. Those clues have fascinated astronomers, Bible scholars, and ordinary people for almost as long as the story has been told.

Matthew tells us that wise men from the East had seen an unusual star that they identified with a newborn "King of the Jews." They called it "his star." This king was so important that the magi planned a long, hard, uncertain journey to find Him. They were not guided by the star to Bethlehem but went, instead, to Jerusalem, the capital city of the Jews, looking for the new king.

Herod (who was the official king of the Jews) and his people were disturbed to hear the wise men's story. Their confusion suggests that they might not have seen the star themselves — that it was only noticed by people like Magi whose job it was to study stars. Herod didn't like the idea of another king in his kingdom, and he ordered the Jewish priests to tell him where he could find this new king. The priests told King Herod and the Magi about an Old Testament prediction that a ruler would be born in Bethlehem. And so the Magi traveled about five miles south of Jerusalem to Bethlehem, where they found Jesus. Matthew tells us that as they set out again, they were "overjoyed" to see the star. It sounds almost as though the star had disappeared and then appeared to them again for the last few miles of their journey.

Matthew wrote about the star in a matter-of-fact way until the end of the story when he said that, as the Magi left Jerusalem, the star "went ahead of them" and "stopped over the place where the child was." No ordinary star or planet could lead like that — like a guide with a flashlight directing a group through a dark forest. For this reason, many people believe the star was a miracle star. Certainly God could have used a supernatural phenomenon to guide

Handel often played the organ in performances at Covent Garden Theatre, London

the Magi. Others have thought that the star's appearance was a natural rather than a supernatural event — that God used ordinary circumstances to work His will.

One of the oldest and most popular of the natural explanations for the star suggests that it was not a star at all, but a close meeting of two planets as they traveled in their regular orbits. Astronomers call that a "conjunction." Around the time that Jesus was born, there was a very rare triple conjunction of Jupiter and Saturn (three meetings in about a year's time). The triple meeting fits many of the clues given in Matthew's gospel. For example, the series of three conjunctions could explain why the wise men seemed to have first seen the star in their homeland, then along the way, and then again after they left Jerusalem.

What did those travelers from the East really see? Was the star's appearance a special miracle, or was it a comet, supernova, star giant, fireball, group of planets, or something else? All of the theories fit part of the clues, some better, some worse. But no theory fits them all.

In spite of all the uncertainty about what the star was, it is very certain what the star meant. It was something God used to bring wealthy, powerful, highly educated men to meet a baby in Bethlehem. Whatever the Magi saw in the sky filled them with a great longing to find the King of kings. From the first time that they saw His sign, they worked and waited with joy and hope for the fulfillment of their search. In that time, the star — His star, the glory of the Lord — was revealed to just a few wise men. That star marked the advent of the birth of Jesus.

There is another advent, though, another coming. The Bible says that Jesus will come again a second time. The Second Advent won't be marked with a star seen by just a few people. When Jesus comes again, the whole sky will be filled with His glory, and all of humanity will see it together.

For now we are imperfect people living in an imperfect world. All of creation, and we ourselves, groan inside, longing for our salvation. It is coming.

This is our hope. After all, "The mouth of the Lord hath spoken it."

This entry is accompanied by track 3 on the CD.

The Legend of the Flying Snakes

*"Thus saith the Lord of hosts; Yet once a little while, and
I will shake the heavens and the earth; the sea, and the
dry land: And I will shake all nations; and the desire of
all nations shall come. The Lord whom ye seek shall suddenly come to His temple, even the Messenger of the
covenant, whom ye delight in: Behold He shall come,
saith the Lord of hosts."*
— based on Haggai 2:6-7; Malachi 3:1

Ubar, the mysterious, the magnificent, an ancient Arabian city, has been
almost forgotten for thousands of years. It has vanished under the
shifting desert sands. This city that was once a fabulously wealthy
trading center became only a legend told by camel drivers whispering beside
their nighttime campfires. Long ago, the whole world knew of Ubar. Caravan
routes from many lands met at her doors. The world came to Ubar because of
its trees — trees that produced the rare and costly spice called frankincense or
olibanum.

Four hundred years before Christ was born, a Greek writer named
Herodotus told this strange story about the frankincense trees. "Arabia is . . .
the only country that produces frankincense. The trees which bear the frankincense are guarded by winged serpents, small in size, and of varied colors,
whereof vast numbers hang about every tree."

Perhaps it was the rulers of ancient Ubar who started the flying snake story
to scare robbers who might want to steal frankincense. A pound of it was worth
as much as gold in those times. People in Egypt, Africa, Arabia, and Palestine
used it as perfume or medicine or burned it to produce a sweet, heavy smell
during religious ceremonies. As a medicine, frankincense was rumored to
smooth wrinkles, soothe muscles, cure toothaches, stop bleeding, and help just
about any ailment that needed curing.

Some of its benefits may have been real. Modern science has discovered that
frankincense has aspirin-like qualities. But it was more than its curative powers that made frankincense so treasured by the ancients. The smell of its burning covered the odors of death and decay and dirt. The sweet perfume of smok-
ing frankincense was valued by many different societies for use in their sacred
rituals.

The small, crooked gum tree that produces frankincense grew in only a few

Frankincense, presented on a golden platter by one of the wise men,
as imagined by Jerome Bosch

places. Scientists call it *Boswellia sacra.* The rulers who owned the trees were very careful about how the frankincense was collected. The harvesters had to belong to official families who were considered better than ordinary people. At the shipping centers, security was tight. Sometimes workers had to wear specially marked clothing. The clothing was taken off and checked at the end of the day to make sure that no stolen frankincense was hidden inside.

Then and now, harvesters collect frankincense by peeling back the bark from the tree and cutting a deep slice into the tree trunk. (Herodotus said that the gatherers first had to use smoke to drive the snakes away!) A milk-like sap oozes from the cut. After a few months, the drippings harden into teardrop-shaped pieces of yellowish frankincense. The purest and most valuable chunks appear only after several cuttings. They are near the cut and are almost white. In fact, the Hebrew word for frankincense means "white." Pieces of it burn with a white fire. In old French it was called *franc encens* — superior incense.

Long before Jesus was born in Bethlehem, God told the Jewish people to burn frankincense in His tabernacle. It was one of four ingredients in a fragrant incense that was dedicated to God — set apart only for use in worship. Anyone who used the holy incense for his or her own enjoyment was to be "cut off" from the rest of the community. "Consider it holy to the Lord," God told them

(Exodus 30:37).

Frankincense was a sign and a reminder to everyone that God is holy. The wise men who followed the star to find baby Jesus gave Him frankincense as a gift. Their costly offering reminds us that Jesus is the mighty, holy God. He is pure and bright, set apart from us, and above us. Today's reading tells us that, one day, the Lord God will come again to His temple and to this world. As the smell of incense once filled the ancient tabernacle, the glory of the Lord's presence will one day fill the world. He is called the "desire of all nations" and the "Messenger of the covenant." These are titles for Messiah, the Holy One of Israel. His presence will shake the nations and bring joy to His people. Once, He came to earth as a baby. Today, He can come to live in people's hearts. One day, Jesus will come again in all His holiness and with power and glory to shake up the whole world.

This entry is accompanied by track 4 on the CD.

Why?

"But who may abide the Day of His coming? And who shall stand when He appeareth? For He is like a refiner's fire."

— based on Malachi 3:2

This is not a good story. It has, for now, no happy ending. It is a story that begins with a lie and ends with murder. It is the Christmas story that no one tells — the story of Herod, king in Jerusalem when Jesus was born.

Jerusalem was the capital of Judea, the land of the Jews. This Herod was called "Herod the Great" because he was the first of the Herodian family line to rule as "King of the Jews." His Judean subjects did not want Herod to be their king. At first, they hated him because of who he was. Later they learned to hate him because of his cruelty. The true kings of Judea were members of the Hasmonean family. Herod was not a Hasmonean. Worse, he was an Edomite, a descendent of Esau. The Jewish people were descendants of Jacob (Esau's twin brother) and so they considered Edomites, like Herod, to be only "half-Jews."

When the Romans conquered Judea, they wanted to place a king on the throne who would be loyal to Rome. They did not trust the royal Hasmoneans who were the rightful heirs. Instead they chose Herod, whose family was important in the region, to rule the Jews. Herod knew that his power depended on the might of the Roman army and the favor of the Roman Caesars. So he collected their taxes, kept the Judean people under control (sometimes with excessive cruelty), and beautified the land with magnificent building projects.

Herod also did everything in his power to eliminate anyone who might threaten his kingship. In the course of his long reign, he murdered most of the people who were close to him because of his jealous fear that they might steal his throne. He killed his brother-in-law, uncle, favorite wife, mother-in-law, and three of his sons. Herod's murderous ways were so well known that the Roman emperor, Augustus Caesar, made a bad joke of it, remarking that he would rather be Herod's pig *(hus)* than his son *(huios)*.

It is no wonder, then, that Herod was desperately jealous when, toward the end of his life, magi came from another kingdom, asking for information about a newborn "King of the Jews." Herod hid his anger behind the smooth lie that he, too, wanted to worship the new king, if only the wise men could help him find the child.

The Bethlehem massacre as imagined by a 16th century artist

When the wise men escaped without giving him the information he wanted, Herod was furious. He sent out a deadly search warrant. In an effort to destroy the new king who had been born in Bethlehem, Herod ordered his soldiers to murder all the boys in that area who were two years old and under. Herod did not know that Joseph had escaped to Egypt with Mary and Jesus after being warned by an angel to flee from Bethlehem. And so, the innocent baby boys of Bethlehem died.

Why did it happen? Evil did not begin or end with Herod. There always has been and always will be wicked people who destroy the innocent for the sake of their own evil plans. And always, we wonder why such things happen and why they are allowed to go unpunished. This question that so many ask is also asked many times in the Bible. It appears in the Old Testament book of Malachi, just before the verses that include today's reading. The Bible's answer to that question is not an easy one.

The answer does not take away the pain of those who suffer. But the Bible's answer is always the same: God is faithful. God is just. God is in control. It is an answer that Christians accept by faith and in hope, knowing that God did not spare even Himself from suffering and evil.

It is no accident that the Bible tells the story of Herod's treachery along with the story of the birth of Jesus. Jesus was born to save the world from such evil. He was born to die for the sins of the world. He patiently waits for the world to come to repentance. One day He will come to judge the world. On that day, evil will be finally and forever conquered. It will not stand under the fire of God's justice. For those who suffer there is no other hope except in the God of love who will someday make all things right.

This entry is accompanied by track 5 on the CD.

The Fire's Work

"And He shall purify the sons of Levi, that they may offer unto the Lord an offering in righteousness."
— based on Malachi 3:3

The house of King Solomon, son of David, had goldsmiths, goldbeaters, and refiners aplenty. Gold was so abundant in his kingdom that silver had little value — it was said that silver seemed as common as stones. The great and the small came from many lands to ask Solomon for his advice and to listen to his wise words. They paid him in gold for what they heard.

Solomon's trading ships brought back gold from the fabled land of Ophir. Kings paid him tribute in gold from the mines of Egypt, Africa, and Arabia — mines whose locations are lost but whose names remain. Once, perhaps, the goldsmiths knew the whereabouts of the golden lands of Havilah and Sheba, Ophir, and Parvaim.

Certainly, King Solomon's goldsmiths would have known that the gold they prepared and purified for the king's golden throne and for his warriors' golden shields, for his golden goblets and spoons — that very gold had already been refined and separated from tons of rock through natural processes or through the hard labor of thousands and thousands of slaves.

Scattered, far-flung, above and below the earth's surface, gold lay pure, never rusting, bright and shining. It was there in streambeds as golden nuggets, washed up from below the earth's surface and separated from rock and gravel through the tumbling and washing of water. It was there as tiny flakes in the sand or dirt, recovered only by the long, tiring, and dirty work of prospectors who swirled and washed the dirt to separate out the gold. It was there deep below the earth, running through the rock like miniature golden streams. The slaves of Solomon's time could only get it through backbreaking work. In the mines, they broke the rock with hammers or cracked it by throwing water on rock faces that had been heated by fire. Then they pounded and crushed the chunks into tiny pieces that could be washed to separate out the gold.

Even then, the gold that came into King Solomon's workshops was not perfect enough. It was not the "pure gold," the "refined gold" that was required for the most precious works of art and worship. The gold for those pieces had to be purified and refined further until it was entirely gold. Because gold melts easily and is nearly ten times heavier than water, it was purified by fire. The melted gold would sink to the bottom of the cup, and impurities would rise to the top where they could be easily removed.

*Many artists have imagined that the gold presented by the Magi
might have been sculpted*

Like the goldsmiths of Ur, Egypt, Nubia, Troy, and Greece, Solomon's goldsmiths could beat and hammer gold into incredibly thin sheets to cover wood objects so that they looked like solid gold. They could spin pure gold into thin threads and weave it into Solomon's royal robes. The goldsmiths, gold-beaters, and refiners of King Solomon's kingdom spent their lives to bring gold forth in purity, fit for a king's use.

Gold was one of the gifts brought to Jesus by the wealthy magi who followed His star. Gold is valuable because it is rare, beautiful, and hard to mine. If all the purified gold, from all time, were melted together into one cube, it could fit within a baseball diamond.

Gold does not rust or tarnish. The silver jewelry found in ancient tombs is black with tarnish, while the gold objects still shine brightly. Gold can be formed and shaped and stretched like no other metal. A piece of pure gold the size of a sugar cube can be pounded thin enough to cover the floor of a small room or stretched into a thread fifty miles long. With heating and reheating, sil-

ver and iron and copper become unmanageable. Gold can be worked and reworked, melted and remelted, stretched and beaten over and over, and it never loses its glitter or its obedience to the hands of the goldsmith. Gold is found in the dirt. It is made fit for a king through breaking, heating, beating, and stretching.

The apostle Peter, a friend of Jesus, wrote that our faith is of "greater worth than gold." Faith is the only gift we have to offer God. Gold or bribes, He does not need. Faith seems such a poor gift, so little of it pure and so much of it rubble. But God lovingly accepts our gift and makes it an "offering in righteousness." He will purify us as a goldsmith's fire refines gold. He will work for our good through all the sadness and trouble that come into our life and that hurt so much. And, when He has tested us, we will "come forth as gold," pure and precious — not by our power, but through His grace.

"Test me, O Lord."

This entry is accompanied by track 6 on the CD.

Daughter of Her Son

"Behold, a virgin shall conceive, and bear a son, and shall call His name Emmanuel, God with us."
— based on Isaiah 7:14; Matthew 1:23

Amother is holding her baby. She feeds it, cuddles it, and rocks it. She watches and wonders and tries to imagine what will happen to her darling child as it grows up. What could be more ordinary than that? Yet it is so special that a family might fill a whole book with photographs of the new baby with its mother. And a mother will remember those baby-holding days all

Mary with the child by a window – a drawing of
mother and child by Rembrandt

the rest of her life.

The Madonna is holding her baby. Madonna and Child. Mother Mary and baby Jesus. So common. So ordinary. She feeds and cuddles and rocks Him. But when she wonders about her darling child she remembers what angels, shepherds, and kings have said about Him. What did she think about, she who was the first one to ponder the puzzle of all puzzles? She held God in her arms.

The pictures of this mother and child are the most common of all pictures. Everyone has seen them. But they are not ordinary. In them, artists have stretched their imaginations to the limit, trying to paint on canvas or carve in stone the meaning of Emmanuel, God in Mary's arms. God on earth. God like us. God with us.

Some of the earliest pictures show the "Maria lactans," Mary feeding baby Jesus. Thus the artists show He is a real human baby. Other paintings are of the "Madre Pia," Mary praying to her son. In those, the artist emphasizes that the baby is Mary's God. Many pictures show Mary or Jesus holding an apple or orange, reminders of the fruit that Adam and Eve ate, bringing sin into the world. The fruit signified that God forgives sin. Pictures with grapes suggested the wine of communion and Jesus' blood on the cross. The shell of a walnut represented Christ's cross. The red on the face of a goldfinch represented a drop of His blood.

Another kind of artwork shows Mary and Jesus. These works of art are quite different from the Madonna and Child pictures that seem so right for Christmas. They are the Pietàs, named from the Italian word for "pity." They show the sorrow of Mary as she holds, not her baby, but the body of the son who has died on a cross. The most famous Pietà is a statue by the great Michelangelo Buonarroti. It has stood in Saint Peter's cathedral in Rome since 1499, carved by the artist and placed there when he was less than twenty-five years old. He sculpted it from the fine white marble of the quarries of Carrara, Italy. Michelangelo's Pietà is so lovely that another artist from his time had this to say about it: "It is certainly a miracle that a formless block of stone could ever have been reduced to a perfection that nature is scarcely able to create in the flesh."

Some of those who saw the Pietà for the first time complained that Mary's beautiful face looked too young. She looks younger than the son that she holds. Whether Michelangelo meant it or not, others have found a special meaning in Mary's young face. It is the meaning, too, of the body she holds so tenderly in her lap. This meaning of the Pietà is explained best by a line from poet Alighieri Dante. In his poem *Paradiso*, he addresses Mary as "Virgin Mother, daughter of your Son." That is the mystery of Mary's son. The human baby she held in her arms is her Creator and Father. He existed before the dawn of the universe. Every human face is young compared to Him. And because He is God, His death was not a meaningless death. The sorrow of the Pietà was turned to joy for Mary and for all of humanity when her son rose from His grave, conquering death for us all.

This is the heart of Christianity. It is the meaning of the Christmas story. Mary's human baby was the God of salvation for all of mankind. It is the puzzle of puzzles, the miracle of miracles. In its truth we rest all our hopes. God became flesh and lived among us. He sympathizes with our weaknesses because He lived as we live. He is with us as Savior. He is with us as Comforter. He is with us as Guardian and Guide. Baby Jesus, Mary's child, is named Emmanuel, God with us. Hallelujah.

This entry is accompanied by track 7 on the CD.

No Christmas Allowed!

"O thou that tellest good tidings to Zion, get thee up into the high mountain: O thou that tellest good tidings to Jerusalem, lift up thy voice with strength; lift it up, be not afraid: Say unto the cities of Judah, Behold your God. Arise, shine, for thy Light is come, and the glory of the Lord is risen upon thee."
— based on Isaiah 40:9, 60:1

There once was a place where it was against the rules to celebrate Christmas. There was a time when you had to pay a fine if you took a day off from work on December 25. This place that sounds like a country of Scrooges and Grinches was the American colonies during the time of the Pilgrims and Puritans.

The Puritans have gotten a bad reputation in recent years. Most people think of them as a society that dressed in black, lived by strict rules, and never had any fun. And, since the Puritans were the ones who made the anti-Christmas laws, we assume that they must have wanted to ruin everyone else's fun as well. But things are not always what they seem. In this case, it wasn't so much the Puritans who were the problem. Christmas was the problem.

The Christmas that the Puritans knew was not at all like the Christmas we celebrate today. Our family-oriented, "presents for the kids" type Christmas is only about 150 years old. It developed with changing times and with the help of people who wanted to get rid of some of the disturbing customs that had been part of Christmas celebrations for centuries.

In his little book, *A Testimony Against Several Profane and Superstitious Customs Now Practiced by Some in New England*, Increase Mather, a Puritan preacher, discussed the Puritan reasons for not keeping Christmas. He explained that early Christians never celebrated Christmas, that there was no proof that Jesus was born on December 25, and that the date for Christmas Day was chosen to compete with the old pagan Roman celebration of Saturnalia that worshiped false gods. All these things were true, but Increase Mather had a better reason for not celebrating Christmas. As he put it, "The manner of Christmas-keeping, as generally observed, is highly dishonourable to the Name of Christ." And the Puritans were right. Christmas was supposed to celebrate and honor the good tidings of Christ's birth, but for many it became just an excuse to party.

Jerusalem bathed in golden light

For most of its history Christmas was celebrated like a carnival, with dancing, singing, and playacting in the streets. Often the joy of Christ's birth was lost in the thrill of celebration. Sometimes Christmas was a bit like an out-of-control Halloween. Merrymakers dressed in animal costumes, and men dressed as women. People went house to house singing songs and expecting a tip or refreshments at the houses they visited. Sometimes they made trouble if they didn't like the handouts they received.

Celebrations lasted throughout the twelve days of Christmas, and it was a time of overeating, drinking, and gambling. After drinking too much wine or with their faces hidden by masks, people acted in ways they would not normally act. Roving bands of young men threatened people with demands for money and drinks. In medieval times, disorderly crowds elected a "Lord of Misrule," who was a mock king with his court. They ridiculed the authorities and sometimes made fun of the ministers and the customs of the churches.

This was the sort of Christmas that the Pilgrims and Puritans remembered from England. When they came to the New World to set up a Christian community, they wanted no part of such practices. They had made a promise to each other to be a "City on a Hill." Just as the lights of a mountaintop city show the way to travelers at night, so the Puritans wanted to be a light to the world, showing God's love and power to change sinners into children of God. It took strength and courage to cross an ocean and attempt to live out that promise in a strange and dangerous land.

If Increase Mather or others of those colonists were with us today, we might argue with them that they went overboard in outlawing Christmas. We could tell them that Christmas can be kept in a way that honors God. But they might notice that we have added the new customs of overshopping, overworking, and overspending to the older Christmas customs of overeating and overdrinking.

There have always been two ways of keeping Christmas. One is just a celebration and nothing more. The other way is the Puritan way — a celebration that honors God. This is the sort of celebration that Isaiah described in today's reading. "Behold your God!" Pay attention to what He has done for you. Arise and shine like a light on a hill. Tell the good news that a Savior is born.

This entry is accompanied by track 8 on the CD.

Who Were They?

"For behold, darkness shall cover the earth, and gross darkness the people; but the Lord shall arise upon thee, and His glory shall be seen upon thee. And the Gentiles shall come to thy light, and kings to the brightness of thy rising."

— based on Isaiah 60:2-3

The cathedral is massive and intricate, one of the largest in all of Europe. Rising above the Rhine River in Cologne, Germany, its twin towers seem to soar to the sky. The stained glass windows, decorations, and carvings seem without end. Inside, behind glass on the high altar, stands a gigantic and magnificent casket, itself shaped like a cathedral, decorated with Bible scenes and covered with gold, silver, and jewels. The casket is the reason that the cathedral was built. It is said that this box holds the bones of the Magi — the wise men who brought gifts to the child Jesus in Bethlehem. In 1164, King Frederick Barbarossa of Germany stole the bones from Milan, Italy, and brought them to Cologne.

Where these relics of the Magi were before Italy is a mystery, but the Cologne Cathedral has this story about them: "Having undergone many trials and fatigues for the gospel, the three wise men meet in Sewa [in Turkey] in A.D. 54 to celebrate the feast of Christmas. Thereupon, after the celebration of Mass, they died: St. Melchior on January 1, aged 116; St. Balthasar on January 6, aged 112; and St. Gaspar on January 11, aged 109."

This story is like many stories about the wise men. It mentions details that are not included in the Bible record (Matthew, chapter 2) of the Magi. Matthew does not provide their names, number, nationality, or age. He doesn't say they traveled on camels or that they were kings. He doesn't explain what magi were. And, despite what we see on Christmas cards and in crèche displays, the Bible does not picture the wise men and shepherds gathered together in a stable. Instead, Matthew says that the Magi found Jesus and his family in a "house." They probably came several months after the shepherds did. Jesus was probably a toddler at the time, since King Herod tried to kill him by ordering the deaths of boys who were two years old and under ("in accordance with the time he had learned from the Magi," v. 16).

We are so used to calling them "the three wise men" that it is hard to imagine that there might have been more or fewer than that. In earlier centuries,

pictures and writings included two, four, eight, twelve, or fourteen Magi. Over time, three gifts/three Magi became the most popular version.

Around six hundred years after Christ's birth, western Christians were calling the wise men Melchior, Gaspar, and Balthasar. One early historian described Melchior as an old white-haired man with a long beard, Gaspar as young and reddish with no beard, and Balthasar as black with a heavy beard. In the east, the Magi were given various other names, including Yazdegerd, Karsudas, and Bithisarea.

What were these "Magi from the east," and where in the east did they come from? The earliest Christian writers thought they were from Arabia, because the gifts that they brought were produced in that area. Most likely the Magi who met Jesus were from Persia or Babylon, which are modern day Iran and Iraq.

The Magi could have been priestly philosopher-thinkers, followers of Zoroaster, the founder of an ancient Persian religion. The prophet Daniel knew such magi. They were the wise men of the Babylonian kingdom who tried to interpret some of their king's dreams. Bible translators have called the group who visited Jesus by different names, including magi, magicians, astrologers, or wise men. They were probably all of these things. They may have practiced the science or magic of the day. They were educated. They studied the stars. They were wealthy.

Christian teachers have always thought that the Magi were Gentiles, not Jews. In this way, one meaning of their visit is to represent the revelation of Jesus as the Messiah for all peoples, Gentiles as well as Jews. That is why some pictures show the Magi each with a different nationality or skin color. The details of Matthew's story certainly fit the idea that Jesus, "the King of the Jews," was also King and Savior of the Gentiles. This is what Isaiah prophesied: "Nations will come to your light."

Whatever and whoever the magi were, they were wise. They were wise enough to know their need, courageous enough to seek, and humble enough — intelligent, rich, and powerful though they were — to fall on their faces to worship their Savior. The light of the star that they followed so faithfully and so far led them to Jesus, the Light of the World.

There is no intellect so great, no curiosity so burning, no dream so desirable that it is not satisfied in Jesus. There is no sin so gross as to prevent His pardon. There is no darkness so deep that the brightness of His light cannot penetrate. Follow in the steps of the wise men and find your satisfaction and salvation.

This entry is accompanied by track 9 on the CD.

Light

*"The people that walked in darkness have seen a great
light; and they that dwell in the land of the shadow of
death, upon them hath the light shined."*
— based on Isaiah 9:2

L et there be light," we demand at Christmas. And in every household that celebrates Christmas and in every store that sells to Christmas shoppers, there is light. Homes and malls are decorated inside and out with blinking bulbs of all kinds imaginable. Many people mark the days in Advent using a wreath with four candles, lighting one candle each week of the four weeks before Christmas.

Christmas in every country and in every time has included light — candles and fires, burning logs, or electric wonders. Light is the essence of life and the symbol of joy and safety. It is no accident that Jesus is called the "Light of the World," nor is it an accident that His birthday is marked by a universal display of light.

The study of the nature of light has occupied the greatest minds that humanity has known — Galileo, Isaac Newton, Albert Einstein, and many others. Their studies explain much, yet they leave much that is not understood. To know a little about light is to know a little about time and space, energy, and matter. To know about light is also to know a little about what God is like. Light is the symbol the Bible uses over and over to describe Him.

The New Testament book of 1 Timothy tells us that God "lives in unapproachable light." Those words suggest that we cannot know all there is to know about God or approach Him as equals. The mysteries surrounding the God of light are represented in the mysteries surrounding the nature of light.

Light is the fastest thing there is. It travels at a speed of 186,282 miles per second. (That's equal to about eight times around the world in one second.) Scientists have concluded that if people could travel at near the speed of light, time would slow down for them and they would get heavier. Knowing the truth of these astounding possibilities doesn't make it any easier to understand them. Our everyday ways of understanding nature are not enough to explain light. How then can we possibly expect to explain all there is to know about God?

Experiments have also shown another surprising characteristic of light. Light acts like two completely different things. It moves like a continuous wave, similar to a steady ripple that comes from a pebble dropped in a pond.

"The Light of the World" – a famous Victorian painting of Jesus

Light is also totally unlike a wave, moving in little bits similar to a line of individual bullets shot from a machine gun. We can accept the truth of this seeming contradiction because it explains the observed facts about light. In the same way, Christians accept the spiritual mystery that God can be both a human baby and the all-powerful God at the same time.

Anyone who has seen a rainbow after a storm sees the individual colors of light as it passes through the raindrops in the sky. This is the light we can see. But there are other kinds of light just as real: the X rays and cosmic rays that can destroy, the radio waves that carry our favorite songs, the microwaves that cook our food. All of these are light energy. We know they are real by their actions just as we know the reality of our invisible God by His activity in our lives.

Light is the source of life itself. Light warms our body with the heat that makes our blood flow and our muscles move. The sunlight that shines on our green planet enters leaf and plant where it is changed, by the miracle of photosynthesis, into the living food energy that every animal and human must have to stay alive. So we can say that light is in every life giving bite of food that we put into our mouths. The Bible tells us that "God is light," and that "in him we live and move and have our being" (1 John 1:5; Acts 17:28). He is, in a sense, the light that keeps us alive.

God showed Himself to Moses in a burning bush. He led the Israelites through the desert by a pillar of fire. The apostle Paul found his Savior in a blinding flash of light. Christ's birth was announced by angels in a glory of light, and the wise men followed the light of a star. God is light. And just as every young child cries for the light that will take away the night fears, so every human heart longs for the light of God's love, every mind searches for the light of God's truth, and every spirit cries for the salvation to lighten its darkness.

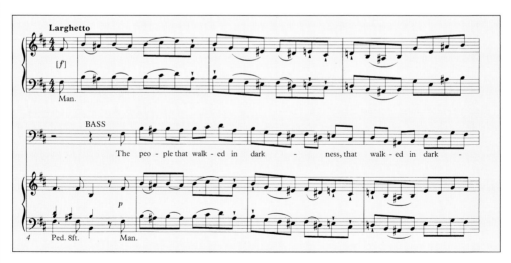

This entry is accompanied by track 10 on the CD.

54

She Wrapped Him in Swaddling Clothes

"For unto us a Child is born, unto us a Son is given; and the government shall be upon His shoulder; and His name shall be called Wonderful, Counsellor, The Mighty God, The Everlasting Father, The Prince of Peace."
— based on Isaiah 9:6

And she . . . wrapped him in swaddling clothes, and laid him in a manger" (Luke 2:7 KJV). That's what Mary did for newborn Jesus. She wrapped him up and put him to bed in an animal's feedbox. Many artists have painted that scene. Others have carved Mary and Joseph and baby Jesus out of wood or stone. But what about the swaddling clothes? Sometimes Jesus is shown wearing no clothes at all. Sometimes He is covered with a cloth blanket or wears something that looks like a nightgown. Japanese artists show him wearing Japanese clothes. African, Russian, Italian, Indian, and South American artists show Jesus wearing African, Russian, Italian, Indian, or South American clothes. Only sometimes does the artist carve or paint Jesus wearing His swaddling clothes.

If you've ever seen an Egyptian mummy, you have a good idea what swaddling clothes look like. Long strips of cloth, which could be as long as a room, were wrapped around and around the baby. Often, the baby's arms were pinned to its sides and its legs kept straight together. Sometimes the bands wound around its chin and forehead so that all you could see were a pair of eyes. In Bible times, the newborn baby was washed clean and rubbed with salt or washed in salt water before it was wrapped up. People thought that the salt helped to harden the baby's skin and make it strong.

Swaddling clothes or swaddling bands were also called "clouts" in the Middle Ages. These names all come from the word for "bandage." Wrapping and binding and bandaging babies has been a tremendously popular method of infant care for thousands of years. It was a custom in many different countries long before Christ was born. Swaddling was not a sign of poverty. It was a sign that the parents loved their baby and knew how to take proper care of it. The Old Testament prophet Ezekiel described an unloved and neglected baby as one who had nobody to wash and salt it and wrap it in swaddling clothes.

Not everyone wrapped babies in the mummy style. In some societies, babies were swaddled loosely, perhaps against a soft pillow. In others, the children were attached to a board or a basket with strips of cloth or leather, to be car-

The shepherds gather around the baby wrapped in swaddling clothes

ried papoose-style. In European countries, swaddling lost its popularity only a few hundred years ago, perhaps because of the new ideas about personal freedom. But some form of swaddling has never been out of fashion.

Today there are still places where parents wrap up their babies in cradles, baskets, boards, or slings. Even in modernized countries, a doctor might suggest soothing a fussy baby by swaddling it in a blanket. Every parent who holds a crying baby close or offers to tuck a worried child into bed quiets the child in a swaddling way.

There are lots of reasons people thought it was a good idea to tightly swaddle their infants with long strips of cloth. Many thought it made the baby strong and helped to straighten its legs and body. An old-time expert wrote, "[The child] must be . . . swaddled to give his little body a strait figure, which is most decent and convenient for a Man and to accustom him to keep upon the feet, for else he would go upon all four [feet] as most Animals do." Other opinions were that swaddling kept babies from hurting themselves, kept them warm, or made them easy to carry. Everywhere, parents swaddled their babies because they loved them and wanted to protect them.

Swaddling is a loving act, but it also means to tie up, control, hold down, restrict, and restrain. And . . . can you imagine? God was swaddled! Today's reading tells us that the Son of God is the greatest of the great. He is a prince in charge of all governments. He is mighty and wonderful and everlasting. This very God became very man, a baby who was wrapped in swaddling clothes. In His human birth, Jesus put aside His power and glory. He became "swaddled" — humble and human and restricted. The Wonderful One lived the life of a commoner. The Supreme Counselor was silent before His accusers. The Mighty God did not call His army of angels to save Him from the cross. The Everlasting Father was an obedient son. The Prince of Peace was wounded for our sins. All this, Jesus did for us and our salvation. King of kings. Lord of lords. Swaddled baby.

This entry is accompanied by track 11 on the CD.

Christmas Angels

"There were shepherds abiding in the field, keeping
watch over their flock by night. And lo, the angel of the
Lord came upon them, and the glory of the Lord shone
round about them, and they were sore afraid."
— based on Luke 2:8-9

What does an angel look like? In movies and on television they sometimes look like ordinary people. They seem to spend their time on earth doing good deeds, maybe trying to "earn their wings." In paintings angels sometimes appear as lovely women with full-length, feathery white wings or as chubby, winged babies hovering in the air like bumblebees.

The angels we hear about today or see in pictures are nothing like real angels. Angels are mentioned often throughout the entire Bible, but not as beautiful women or fat infants or good humans turning into something better. The best description of real angels is that they are awesome. Those who met angels had no doubt that they had met messengers from God.

Although angels usually appeared in human shape (and without wings), they almost always terrified the people who saw them. Before an angel could announce God's message, it must calm its listeners. "Don't be afraid" were usually the first words out of an angel's mouth. Such kind words are a comfort from these mighty creatures that the Bible tells us guard, defend, and take care of God's people.

Angels are not equal to God. They are not like humans, and people do not turn into angels when they die. Angels were created by God, just as humans were. Angels are God's servants and God's messengers. They form His army, and there are countless numbers of them. Angels carry out God's judgment; He uses them to battle evil and punish evildoers. He also uses them to help and protect believers.

When angels appear in human form, they always look like men, never like women or children. But since Jesus said that angels do not marry, we assume that they are not divided into sexes as humans are. They are spirit beings, not bodily beings like humans. They show themselves with wind and fire and brilliant light. Angels are powerful, but not all-powerful. They are intelligent, but not all-knowing. The Bible says that God's people will one day judge the angels.

Many religions and cultures have tried to discover the details of angelic

The angel of the Lord, bearing tidings of great joy, has been imagined in many different and often fanciful ways

names, jobs, and categories. Most of these attempts are just fancy guesses. One popular system devised by Christian scholars in the Middle Ages claimed that there were nine choirs of angels in three groups of three. From highest to lowest, the ranks were given as seraphim, cherubim, thrones, dominions, virtues, powers, principalities, archangels, and angels.

The Bible describes seraphim as creatures with six wings. They stand near God's throne and praise His holiness and power. The cherubim of the Bible are as different from the cherubs on Valentine's Day cards as anything could be. The prophet Ezekiel saw them in a vision of God's majesty as they held up His throne. They appeared in a windstorm, with clouds and flashing lightning. Each of the cherubim had four wings, two human hands, and four faces — the face of a man, the face of a lion, the face of a bull, and the face of an eagle. The beating of their wings sounded like a waterfall or the screaming of a battle.

The prophet Daniel was visited several times by angels. His description of an angel is one of the most detailed in the Bible: "There before me was a man dressed in linen, with a belt of the finest gold around his waist. His body was like chrysolite [a golden stone], his face like lightning, his eyes like flaming torches, his arms and legs like the gleam of burnished bronze, and his voice like the sound of a multitude" (Daniel 10:5-6).

Two angels are named in the Bible: Gabriel and the archangel Michael.

Michael is a prince among angels and the protector of Israel. He leads God's armies in battle. Gabriel is a messenger from God to His servants. It was Gabriel who announced the birth of Jesus' cousin John to Zechariah, John's father. Gabriel also told Mary that she would be the mother of Jesus.

Perhaps it was Gabriel who warned the Magi to escape from Herod. An angel also appeared four times to Joseph in dreams, to tell him what he should do. And an angel appeared with "a great company" of the heavenly angel army to tell the good news of Jesus' birth to the shepherds. Eight times angels appear in the Christmas story. They are part of almost every event that is told of Jesus' birth.

A king's birth is usually marked by ceremony, celebration, and riches. The birth of the King of kings was noticed by animals and shepherds, a humble mother, and her carpenter husband in the quiet of a stable. The Christmas angels were the sign that His birth was not at all what it seemed to be. The Christmas angels delivered a message that witnesses to all of creation across all of time. That day, in the city of Bethlehem, Jesus Christ was born. He is Lord of the universe, Creator of the angels, and humanity's dear Savior. Well did the angels shout, "Glory to God in the Highest."

This entry and the following one are accompanied by track 12 on the CD.

The Christmas Day Mystery

"And the angel said unto them, Fear not; for behold, I
bring you good tidings of great joy, which shall be to all
people: For unto you is born this day, in the City of
David, a Saviour, which is Christ the Lord."
— based on Luke 2:10–11

For unto you is born this day . . . a Saviour, which is Christ the Lord"
Luke 2:11 KJV). When the shepherds heard this announcement from the
angel choir, they rejoiced because that very day, in their own lifetimes,
something incredible had happened. A Savior had been born. What day of the
week or month that was could not have mattered to them. Nowadays, most
people assume that Jesus was born on December 25 in the year one. But, in
fact, we don't know the exact day of Christ's birth. We don't know the month.
We don't even know the year.

The very first Christians did not celebrate Christmas. For them, Easter was
the most important observance, because it marked the death and resurrection
of Jesus. It wasn't until about four hundred years after Jesus was born that
Christians began to celebrate His birthday. At that time many different dates
were suggested as the correct one, including March 28, November 18, and
January 6. Some eastern churches still celebrate Christmas on January 6,
which is also a remembrance of the visit of the magi.

No one is certain why December 25 was chosen as the date of Christ's birth.
It used to be a common belief that important events happened on the same day
in different months. Since some people thought that Jesus died on March 25,
it made sense to them that He was also born on a twenty-fifth (but of
December). It is also very possible that the choice of December 25 was simply
a way of dealing with new Christians who still wanted to enjoy the Roman celebration of Saturnalia in mid-December. Perhaps church leaders hoped to limit
some of the wilder parts of that holiday by making December 25 a Christian
celebration instead of a pagan one.

In modern times, historians, astronomers, and Bible scholars have continued to try to calculate the exact day, month, and year that Christ was born.
Although there are good estimates for the correct year, ideas about the month
and day are only guesswork. The Bible does not tell us the month and day that
Jesus was born. Guessing them depends on putting together clues (from
ancient stories or from other events in Christ's life) like pieces in a puzzle.

The area called Shepherds Fields outside Bethlehem

For example, those shepherds who heard the angel tell them "unto you this day" were watching their flocks outside at night. What time of year did shepherds stay outside guarding their sheep? Some say it was only in spring when there were new lambs. Others think that the sheep near Bethlehem were used for temple sacrifices in Jerusalem, so those shepherds may have been outside with their sheep all year round. There probably are as many theories for the

Christmas date as there are people who have tried to guess it. Like the ideas about the sheep, the theories are mostly a matter of opinion.

The gospels of Matthew and Luke do mention some events that suggest the year of Christ's birth. Matthew tells us that Jesus was born while Herod the Great was king in Jerusalem. Herod probably died in 4 B.C. Luke tells us that Jesus was born when the Roman emperor Caesar Augustus had ordered a census and while Quirinius was the governor of Syria. The dates for the census and for Quirinius are not certain, but the suggested timing of these historical events puts the birth of Christ somewhere between 1 and 10 B.C.

If it seems confusing that Christ was born in a B.C. (before Christ) year, rather than the year A.D. 1 ("in the year of the Lord"), we can partly blame a monk by the name of Dionysius Exiguus. He made an error of about four years in his calculations for the calendar he invented that counts years (B.C. or A.D.) from the birth of Christ.

The shepherds did not care what day it was that Christ had come among them — only that He had come. It was not "what day" that mattered to them, but "this day." "This" was the day that a Savior had been born. "This" was the day to rejoice. "This" was the day to meet Him. "This" was the day to spread the good news. It is the same for us. "Now is the day of [our] salvation." The date for Christmas matters little. Christmas day, this day, and every future day we have a Savior with us. This is the day to meet Him. This is the day to spread the good news. This is the day of the Lord. "Let us rejoice and be glad in it."

This entry and the previous one are accompanied by track 12 on the CD.

The Carol Quiz

*"And suddenly there was with the angel a multitude of
the heavenly host, praising God, and saying, Glory to
God in the highest, and peace on earth, good will
towards men."*
— based on Luke 2:13-14

In 1679, at a point where the waters of Lake Huron meet the waters of Lake Michigan, Huron Indians celebrated Christmas. The people paraded to church. A man led the way holding a star high on a long pole. Three chiefs acted the parts of the Magi and carried polished shells as gifts for Jesus.

It was the Huron who probably sang the first carol ever heard in North America. More than thirty years before that Christmas celebration, the missionary priest Father Jean de Brebeuf wrote a carol for the Huron in their own language. He called it "Jesous Ahatonhia." Nowadays it is known as "The Huron Carol." Father de Brebeuf belonged to the "Society of Jesus" (the Jesuits). He was a man of great strength, courage, and sweetness. He spent almost twenty-five years living among the Huron near Quebec. Father de Brebeuf once wrote that the reason he had left his home in France to live in the New World was so that he could "proclaim the true God and his son, Jesus Christ" to the Hurons that he loved "as brothers."

A fanciful English translation of "The Huron Carol" is called "'Twas in the Moon of Winter Time." It describes the wise men as "hunter braves" and baby Jesus as wrapped in a robe of rabbit skin. The original title of the carol means "Jesus, He Is Born." Like other carols, old and new, it tells simply the Christmas story of angels, the star, and the wise men. And, as has been done with many other carols, Father de Brebeuf chose an old tune to accompany his words, in this case a sixteenth-century French carol called "A Young Maid."

Unlike more solemn and complicated religious music, carols have always been the popular, simple songs of ordinary people. In some periods of centuries past, carol singing was a little too popular and, for some, was associated with disorder, rowdiness, and the wilder parts of Christmas celebrations.

Caroling is said to have begun in the thirteenth century with the songs of Saint Francis of Assisi, the Roman Catholic priest famous for his love of animals. In England during the next few centuries, caroling was extremely popular. That period might be called the golden age of carols. We still sing some of the same carols today. "God Rest Ye Merry, Gentlemen" and "O Come, O

Come, Emmanuel" are both ancient carols. The words for other carols were written in more modern times but use old melodies. "What Child Is This?" was written in 1865, but the music is "Greensleeves," a tune that is older than Shakespeare.

For some carols, both the words and music were written in more recent times. A good example is "Hark! The Herald Angels Sing," written by the great evangelical preacher Charles Wesley. He probably has the all-time record for hymn writing — more than 6,500 songs. The music for Wesley's carol was written by the famous composer Felix Mendelssohn. He originally wrote the music for a celebration of the invention of the printing press and once said that his melody would "never do to sacred words." Mendelssohn would be very surprised that it has become part of a popular carol.

One of the Christmas carols from the 1800s is unusual because the author wrote it after the terrible experiences of wartime. The great poet Henry Wadsworth Longfellow wrote "I Heard the Bells on Christmas Day" after his son was wounded during the United States Civil War. In his carol Longfellow described how the war almost made him give up hope until he remembered that "God is not dead, nor doth He sleep." His carol ends with the sureness and hope that God will, one day, bring peace to earth.

No matter when or why they were written, many Christmas carols are reminders of the very first carol spoken by angels to the shepherds, long ago

near Bethlehem. Christmas carols retell, in many different styles and ways, that old, old song of the angels. Glory to God. Peace. Joy. That is the message, too, of the six carols in today's story. The songs are from different times, places, and peoples. But separately or together, they all tell the same story of joy that Christ is born.

Here, once more, we retell the Christmas story through carols. You might like to take the challenge of this "Carol Quiz" and match each line below with one of the carols mentioned above (answers in the "Read More About It" section at the back of the book).

"Rejoice! Rejoice! Emmanuel shall come to thee."
"This, this is Christ the King."
"Glory to the newborn King."
"Peace on earth, good will to men."
"Jesus, He is born."
"O tidings of comfort and joy."

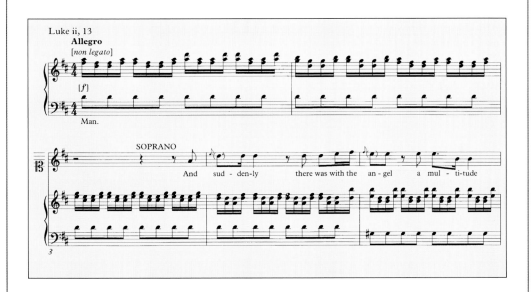

This entry is accompanied by track 13 on the CD. (Note: Track 12 flows into track 13.)

These Tired Eyes, These Wrinkled Hands

"Rejoice greatly, O daughter of Zion, shout, O daughter
of Jerusalem; behold, thy King cometh unto thee: He is
the righteous Saviour; and He shall speak peace unto the
heathen."
— based on Zechariah 9:9-10

Anna and Simeon had been watching, hoping, expecting — waiting for a long, long time. Even so, they might not quite have expected it when the day arrived. The day their watching and waiting were over, the day their hopes were finally satisfied, was the day that Mary and Joseph brought their six-week-old son to the temple at Jerusalem.

That day must have been like almost any day. People were coming and going. The rich and the poor were there. Worshipers prayed or gave their offerings. They took part in ceremonies just as they did on other days. Anna, who prayed there every day, and Simeon, who was faithful in worship, could not have guessed that what they were waiting for had finally come without warning.

Those two were old with waiting. Anna had seen more than eighty-four years pass by. She was a daughter of the tribe of Asher. Some said that women of that tribe were the prettiest of all. But her beauty was long gone. Once she had been a wife, but her husband had died after they were together only seven years. If she had children, even they were old by now. Anna continued to wait. She waited with weary eyes and shaking hands for the Messiah who had been promised to Israel. She spent every day and every night in the temple praying and fasting.

Simeon waited also. He was known in Jerusalem for his goodness and fairness and for his faithfulness in worship at the temple. God had promised him that before he died, he would see Messiah, the comfort of Israel, with his own eyes. Simeon waited with the faithfulness of a good servant at the door of his master's house or a soldier on watch at a fortress gate.

It was Simeon who saw Jesus first, as Mary and Joseph brought Him to the temple courts to complete the ceremonies required for a newborn child. Mary had waited the necessary forty days before bringing an offering for her ceremonial purification after the birth of a son. Did Simeon even notice the offering Mary and Joseph brought? It was only two small pigeons or doves, the very least allowed. Those who could afford it were required to bring a year-old

"My eyes have seen your salvation" was old Simeon's cry of joy upon seeing the baby

lamb plus a young pigeon or dove for the purification sacrifice. The wealthier parents who brought the more expensive gifts would have paid little notice to the family with only two pigeons and a babe in hand. They might have been surprised to see Simeon rush up and gather that child in his arms. They would have been astounded to hear Simeon announce that this baby was the glory of Israel and the Savior of the world.

Was Simeon crying with joy when he praised the Lord and told everyone that God had kept His promises? "Now I can die in peace," he shouted. "My eyes have seen Your salvation." Somewhere, from inside the temple or another section of its courts, Anna must have heard the commotion. At the very moment when Simeon was singing praises, the prophetess Anna came up to join them. In the time it takes to turn a corner, look up, or walk a few halting steps, she found that her prophecies had finally come to their end. Like Simeon, she began to thank God. The thanks must have broken forth from inside her like the water breaks from a dam that is almost overflowing, a dam that the gatekeepers have waited too long to open. She could not stop thanking God. She could not stop talking.

There were others like her and like Simeon who were also waiting for the Messiah. To all these, she told the story of the Christ she had seen with her tired old eyes, the Savior she had touched with her wrinkled and crooked old hands. There they stood that day. An old man. An old woman. If they had ever doubted, if they had ever grown weary with waiting and wondering about the truth of God's promises, they had not turned aside from the way of the Lord.

They continued to pray and to hope until they had seen their salvation with their own eyes and had touched Him with their own hands. It came in a moment. It came unexpectedly. "Look, the Lamb of God, who takes away the sin of the world!" (John 1:29). "Even so, come, Lord Jesus" (Revelation 22:20 KJV). We too await You this Advent season.

This entry is accompanied by track 14 on the CD.

A Victorian shoepolish boy touting for business

The Shoepolish Boy

"Then shall the eyes of the blind be open'd, and the ears
of the deaf unstopped; then shall the lame man leap as a
hart, and the tongue of the dumb shall sing."
— based on Isaiah 35:5-6

The boy, Charles, was only twelve years old when his parents sent him to work in the shoepolish factory. "Blacking" they called it back then — black polish for shoes. The factory where Charles worked was black too. It was dark and dirty and falling apart. Big, old gray rats squeaked and scuffled and ran all over the floor while Charles worked with the other children. That was London in 1824, when children from poor families often worked all day to get money for food. Soon after Charles started working, his father was put in jail for not paying his bills. The family needed the six shillings a week that Charles earned at the shoepolish factory. It was less than a dollar in American money, but it would buy him at least one meal a day to help with expenses.

It was Charles's job to package the pots of paste-blacking. He wrapped each jar in oil paper and then in blue paper. He tied them with string and then neatly cut the edges off the paper. Finally, he stuck the company label on top. One of the other boys, an orphan named Bob Fagin, showed Charles how to tie the string around each jar and knot it. Charles did his work pot by pot, hour by hour, day after day. He was miserable. The other boys saw that there was something special about Charles. They called him "the young gentleman," but his own dreams of becoming a "learned and distinguished man" were crushed.

Charles Dickens was wrong about his future. He did grow up to be a distinguished man. Although he became a famous author, he never forgot the blacking factory. Much later, he wrote of that time, saying, "No words can express the secret agony of my soul."

Dickens used the memories of the hard times from his childhood to write his novels. Sometimes he even gave his characters the names or personalities of people from his past. One such story is about an orphan named Oliver Twist. In that book the ringleader of a gang of pickpockets is called Fagin, named after Bob Fagin, the boy from the blacking factory.

Dickens also wrote the very first Christmas book. He called it *A Christmas Carol*, and he finished it in six weeks — just in time for Christmas of 1843. It was published in red and gold with hand-colored drawings and golden edges.

It was a best seller from the start and has been popular ever since.

Scrooge and Tiny Tim and the Ghosts of Christmas keep showing up in movies and on television and even in cartoons and comic books. Dickens's Christmas story is about two kinds of people. Scrooge is rich and healthy, but his heart is sick with meanness and greed. Tiny Tim cannot walk, but his spirit is strong and loving. It is Tiny Tim who knows the true meaning of Christmas right from the beginning. In one part of the story, Tim rides home from Christmas services on his dad's shoulders. The boy tells his father that he hopes the church people will notice his crippled legs because, he says, "it might be pleasant to them to remember, upon Christmas Day, who made lame beggars walk and blind men see."

Tiny Tim's words are a reminder that when Jesus was on earth, He healed the sick and the handicapped and the broken-hearted. This part of Jesus' ministry was prophesied in the verses from the Old Testament that we read today. The One who healed in Israel long ago is still our healer today. The verses promise that someday God will heal His people, body and soul. The blind will see and the deaf will hear. Those who cannot walk will jump high like deer, and those who cannot speak will be able to sing.

Jesus did not come to Bethlehem just to fix broken bodies. He came to redeem our sick hearts. He came for the selfish, miserly, mean-hearted Scrooges. He came to a world crippled by sin. The baby of Bethlehem grew up to be the man of Calvary. There He took upon Himself the sins and sorrows and sickness of all humanity. There He offered to all the gift of healing. No Christmas gift, however wonderful, can satisfy a broken heart, heal a suffering body, or change a sinful life. Only Jesus and His gift of salvation offers that promise: hope and help for our present sorrows and perfect life, health, and pure joy one day in heaven.

This entry is accompanied by track 15 on the CD.

They Fall Down and Can't Get Up Again

"He shall feed His flock like a shepherd: He shall gather
the lambs with His arm, and carry them in His bosom,
and gently lead those that are with young."
— based on Isaiah 40:11

In the pastures and fields, on the hills and in the valleys, wherever sheep go, they need a shepherd. Sheep have no way to protect themselves from lion or wolf or bear. They cannot kick or bite their enemies. They have no claws or sharp teeth to fight with. All that they have is a powerful instinct to stay together with the flock. Sheep run as a group, pressing as close to each other as they can. That is why one small sheepdog can herd a whole flock of sheep. Danger causes the herd to stampede together in a mad dash to get away. But when the sheep are panicked, it is easy for them to hurt themselves. Their herd instinct cannot save them. Sheep need a shepherd.

The shepherd's job is to protect the sheep from themselves and from their enemies. In Bible times, a shepherd carried a heavy club, the "rod," as a weapon to protect his animals. With the wool from his own sheep he formed a pouch with a string on either side. That was the sling with which the shepherd could hurl a rock with deadly accuracy against a lion or bear. With the sling he could also drop a stone in front of a sheep to make it turn away from the places it shouldn't go.

And what of the lost sheep? Separated from the shepherd and from the flock, a lost sheep is in the greatest danger, especially if it has fallen down. A sheep fallen, with its feet off the ground, cannot get itself back up again. That is because sheep have an unusual reflex that causes them to become very still if their feet leave the ground. A fat sheep, one with lots of wool or pregnant, might lie down and accidentally tip over. When that happens the sheep seems to freeze and acts as if it has given up. A fallen sheep is an easy target for attack. Even if a wild animal doesn't get it, the sheep can die from gases that build up inside because of the way it digests food. The shepherd must always be on the lookout for the lost sheep and the fallen sheep. When he finds them, he gently places them on their feet and returns them to the safety of the flock.

Sheep need a shepherd, not just for safety but also for everyday guidance. With his staff to lean on as he walks, a shepherd spends his days leading his flock to the secret watering places in a dry land. He leads them to fresh fields where they can eat grass that has not been trampled and dirtied by daily feed

ing. The shepherd's eyes search for poisonous plants that could injure his sheep, and he prepares a safe spot for them to graze.

At night the shepherd must lead his flock into the safety of the sheepfold. He cannot force the sheep to go ahead of him, because they would fear the enclosure and might run in panic. He goes in front of them, and they follow. As the sheep enter the fold, they pass under the shepherd's staff so he can count them and separate their wool with his staff to look for cuts and injuries. The shepherd covers the wounds with oil to help them heal.

With the loop of his staff, a shepherd might pull a newborn lamb toward its mother to feed. That way the mother learns the smell of its baby and isn't confused by the smell of the shepherd's hands on the wool. Sometimes a mother might give birth to twin lambs and accept only one of them. Then the shepherd has to take the rejected lamb and carry it on his shoulders. He has to feed it himself or trick a ewe that has lost its baby into feeding the new one.

It was shepherds such as these who were startled one night by a sky filled with angels and an invitation to look for a baby in swaddling clothes. "A Savior . . . born to you," the angels told these rough men who lived in the fields with sheep. These shepherds probably knew all the stables in town where such a babe could be found. They would have been comfortable kneeling among the animals to worship the child whom the angels had called "Christ the Lord." The shepherds probably did not know the other name for that baby, but they would have been proud to hear it. Shepherds were the first to meet Jesus, the Great, Good Shepherd.

Here we are, lost sheep in need of a shepherd. We need Jesus. He is the Lord, our Shepherd, who saves us, lifts us up when we fall, and provides all that we need to live.

This entry is accompanied by track 16 on the CD.

The Reindeer People

"Come unto Him all ye that labour and are heavy laden, and He will give you rest. Take His yoke upon you, and learn of Him; for He is meek and lowly in heart: and ye shall find rest unto your souls. His yoke is easy, and His burthen is light."
— based on Matthew 11:28-30

Reindeer are wanderers. In the northernmost lands, near the Arctic Circle, they migrate each fall and spring between inland forest and airy shoreland. In winter they search for shelter and for "reindeer moss," a favorite food. In summer they look for breezy spots where they can avoid the troublesome mosquitoes and flies that tickle their noses and burrow into their skin.

People wander with the reindeer. They herd them, protect them from wolves, drink their milk, and use them for food and to pull their sleds. Others call these people Laplanders. They are the Saami, "the reindeer people," the original inhabitants of the northern sections of Norway, Sweden, Finland, and Russia. Every Saami family knows its own reindeer, even when they are mixed in the herd with others during roundups. The Saami mark the ears of their reindeer with a unique code that they can recognize instantly. Each summer on "calf marking day," the Saami herdsmen cut their own distinct pattern of notches and slits in the ears of the young animals. It is no easy job to separate the babies from their mothers. The Saami do it much like a cowboy brands his cows. They team up to herd, corral, and lasso the young reindeer. Although the different families share the work of herding, the earmarking patterns are not shared. Sometimes, one ear shows which specific person owns the reindeer, while the other ear shows the general family name. It's as if the reindeer were wearing the first and last names of their owners.

The tamest reindeer are called *härks*. A well-trained härk with a bell around its neck is very valuable as a leader. The Saami can guide it with a rope, and all the other reindeer will follow, even into a dark forest where they can't see whether there is danger. The reindeer herd will follow the härk as if they were sheep trotting after a shepherd. Sometimes the herdsman can wear the bell himself and keep his hands free. An especially good lead härk will just follow the sound of the bell. The rest of the herd will calmly come along behind. The Saami call it "following empty."

Just as a sled dog pulls an Eskimo sleigh, the härks are used to pull the Saami sleds. Their sleds, called *pulkas*, have no runners and look like canoes. They slide along the snow as smoothly as a boat slides through water. The reindeer härk (usually only one) is hitched to a pulka with the help of a soft yoke that it wears over its back. A rope runs from the bottom of the yoke, through the back legs of the reindeer, and joins to the front of the sled.

Reindeer are very strong and fast. Their ankles make a strange clicking and snapping sound when they run. Their large, wide hooves support them on the snow and ice and help them to be excellent swimmers. In the days before snow-

Reindeer have always been used to pull sleds by peoples other than the Saami. This picture shows reindeer in St Petersburg, Russia

mobiles and trucks, the Saami had only their reindeer for transportation.

Reindeer can pull heavy loads in a sled for long distances. A single reindeer can pull a burden weighing more than five hundred pounds for forty miles in one day. If a härk has to carry a heavy burden downhill, the Saami will tie another härk to the back of the sled to act as a brake. But if the reindeer has to pull up a steep hill, it has to do so by itself, sometimes dropping to its knees to get that heavy load uphill.

Sometimes humans feel like a härk hooked to a heavy sled. Sometimes their worries and troubles seem to weigh them down. Before Christmas, lots of kids worry about whether they have been "naughty or nice." Christmas or not, though, it is a good thing to consider our wrong deeds and thoughts and to think about our sins. The guilt they bring is the biggest burden anyone ever carries. That is why one of the promises of Jesus is so wonderful. He said, "Come to me, all you who are weary and burdened, and I will give you rest. . . . For my yoke is easy and my burden is light" (Matthew 11:28, 30).

When God forgives us, He takes away the heavy load of our guilt and sin. He lays a new burden on us, the burden of obedience. It is an easy burden because He helps us to carry it. We can bear God's yoke in hope and joy and peace. Then we can follow Jesus like sheep follow the voice of the shepherd and like reindeer follow the bells of the Saami.

Part of the text of this entry is accompanied by track 17 on the CD.

Castle or Cave?

*"He was despised and rejected of men, a man of sorrows,
and acquainted with grief. He gave His back to the
smiters, and His cheeks to them that plucked off the hair:
He hid not His face from shame and spitting. Surely He
hath borne our griefs, and carried our sorrows: He was
wounded for our transgressions, He was bruised for our
iniquities; the chastisement of our peace was upon Him
and with His stripes we are healed."*
— based on Isaiah 53:3; 50:6; 53:4-5

Carlo was a Spanish prince who became ruler of Naples, Italy, in 1734. He grew fascinated with the nativity scenes that the Italians call *presepi*. King Carlo hired the best artists and fashion and scene designers to help him build huge displays around the figures of Mary, Joseph, and Jesus in the stable.

In King Carlo's castle at Christmas, everyone's attention was on the presepio. In fact, Carlo had started a fad. The homes of the nobility also showcased magnificent presepi. The lords and ladies tried to outdo each other. With the start of the Christmas season, the contest was on. Who would have the most beautiful, the biggest, the most expensive, the most elaborate presepio? Each noble family held an open house at Christmas to show off its presepio.

The manger scenes might contain a thousand shepherds plus wise men, animals, and all sorts of miniature figures. There were lords and ladies dressed just like Italian nobility. There might be fishermen fishing, children chasing a dog, or men eating spaghetti. The details were exact down to the wrinkles on the faces and the tiny loaves of bread, sausages, or fruits stacked on miniature store shelves. The scenery could include whole villages, streams with real water, fountains, mountains, castles, and ruins. There might even be a small volcano erupting, a replica of Naples's nearby Mount Vesuvius.

Many of the figures had china heads, wooden arms and legs, and cloth bodies. Inside the tiny dolls were iron wires so that their bodies could be moved and placed in different positions. Queen Maria and her ladies-in-waiting sewed some of the costumes themselves. The dresses were made from the finest fabrics and lace and were trimmed with real jewels, gold, and silver. It is said that one of the wise men wore a perfect little copy of King Carlo's own royal cape.

The splendor of the Italian presepi honored Jesus as the King of kings, but

they were not at all like the place where He was born. The grandness and beauty of King Carlo's nativity scenes had nothing in common with the poverty and simplicity of the stable in Bethlehem. There is no way of knowing what that stable really looked like. It might have been a one-room stone or mud-walled hut behind the inn. It could have been a temporary outdoor animal shelter, set up for those who had come to Bethlehem to register for the census. Most likely, Jesus was born in someone's cave stable. There are many caves in the hills around Bethlehem, and the very earliest references to His birthplace call it a cave.

The place where Jesus was born was the sort of place where a homeless person, an outcast, or a stranger might rest for the night. Jesus was all of those, both at His birth and at His death many years later. He was despised and rejected by many of those He came to save. What, then, could the Italians have been thinking when they designed their gorgeous presepi? Why have many other artists painted or displayed Jesus in magnificence and beauty at His birth? They knew, of course, that it was not the stable that was glorious, but the baby who was born there.

The magnificence of the Italian presepi and the stink of the hay in the real stable are both part of the nativity scene. Both tell the truth about what happened there in Bethlehem. It is the truth that a Bethlehem feedbox held the greatest treasure the world has ever known. The God of the universe was born a human baby in a lowly stable. In *The Everlasting Man*, author G. K. Chesterton suggested the wonder of this truth with these words, "The hands that had made the sun and stars were too small to reach the huge heads of the cattle." So, said Chesterton, "Bethlehem is emphatically a place where extremes meet."

Not only did extremes meet at Bethlehem, but they met at Calvary on the day that Jesus died. Here is what happened to the One who could have called ten thousand angels to His side. He was despised. He was beaten. He was spit on. He was crucified. But that day also, a treasure was secured for us. Our Lord and King experienced our grief. He carried our sorrows. He was wounded for our sin. "The punishment that brought us peace" was put on Him.

Jesus was born in a shelter for animals. He was hated by many during His lifetime. He died a criminal's death. Jesus lived from cave to cross — for us.

This entry is accompanied by tracks 18-20 on the CD.

Perfume of the Pharaohs

*"He was cut off out of the land of the living: For the
transgression of Thy people was He stricken."*
— based on Isaiah 53:8

It is as ancient as the Egyptian pharaohs and as modern as toothpaste. It
was used to bury the dead and to perfume a young maiden. It tastes bitter,
but smells sweet. It is myrrh. It was once the most costly, the most desirable, the most popular of all the ancient spices. Its only rival was frankincense.

*Ancient Egyptian cities, such as the ruins of Philae, are all that remain of the
splendour of the Pharaohs*

It could heal, soothe, beautify, honor, and preserve its users. All this from the oily, brownish drips of a scrubby, scrawny, thorny tree.

Those who collect the once precious myrrh don't even need to work hard to get it. The bark of the tree splits and cracks on its own. It oozes a gummy sap just like a Christmas tree sometimes does. Often the harvesters add their own cuts into the thick bark to release more of the myrrh stored in hidden channels beneath the surface. With time, the gum dries in teardrops of a yellowish- to reddish-brown color. These are scraped off the tree and can be powdered or partly dissolved in oil or alcohol for use in medicines, perfumes, rubbing oils, and incense.

All sorts of myrrh products are still available today, including inexpensive myrrh mouthwashes, chewing gums, toothpastes, and perfumes. You can find capsules and extracts and essential oils of myrrh. Today it is the stuff of uncertain home remedies. For many centuries it was the treasure of kings, so desirable that a pound of it could cost several thousand dollars. The myrrh trees grew in the same few desert places of Arabia and Africa that supplied the ancient world with frankincense. When Joseph of the many-colored coat was sold into slavery by his brothers, it was to a caravan of myrrh traders. The Queen of Saba (Sheba), from southwest Arabia, may have come to visit the great King Solomon of Israel partly to promote the trade of myrrh and frankincense. When the young Jewish girl Esther was preparing to be queen of Persia, she used myrrh for six months as a beauty treatment.

Myrrh means bitter in many languages, but its sweet, powerful odor covers the bitter smells that nothing else can hide. It was a choice body oil, deodorant, and mouthwash for Egyptians, Romans, and Greeks. An old book of medicine from the first century A.D. recommends that myrrh be "chewed for the stinking of the breath," or spread on "for the grief of the arme pitts."

Doctors prescribed myrrh to heal many diseases. They used it to cover the smell of rotting wounds. People suffering from pain chewed or swallowed myrrh. It probably helped. Modern science has confirmed that myrrh can work as a painkiller. If myrrh failed as a treatment for a disease and the patient died, it still was important for the funeral and burial. The perfume of the myrrh hid the odor of death. Kings and pharaohs could afford to have their bodies buried with huge amounts of myrrh and other spices. At his death, King Asa of Israel was laid on a bed of spices in his tomb in the City of David. Egyptians prepared their mummies by putting myrrh and other spices inside the body before wrapping it.

It was natural that the wise men who traveled so far to honor the infant Jesus should give Him gifts fit for a king: gold, frankincense, and myrrh — the treasures of their day. But the same sweet perfume that honored Jesus at His birth would mark His death many years later. No one likes to think about death when a baby is born. But death was the reason for Jesus' birth. Isaiah tells us that He was born to die for the sins of His people. We are His people. For our sakes, He was crucified — taken from the land of the living. After He died, His friends took His body from the cross. One offered a tomb as a gift. Another brought seventy-five pounds of myrrh and other spices. Together they wrapped Christ's body in strips of linen, covered it with spices, and laid it in the cave tomb. The entrance was then sealed with a stone. It was over, they thought.

The Queen of Sheba and Queen Esther, King Solomon, and King Asa still lie in their tombs, awaiting the Day of Judgment. Their bodies may be perfumed, but all the myrrh in the world cannot hide the fact that they are dead, nor can it bring them back to life. But the stone is gone from the doorway of Jesus' tomb. He is not there.

"It was impossible for death to keep its hold on him" (Acts 2:24). He has conquered death for us all. "By his wounds we are healed" (Isaiah 53:5). And because Jesus lives, we know that we shall live also if He is our Savior.

This entry is accompanied by track 21 on the CD.

Lovefeast

"How beautiful are the feet of them that preach the
gospel of peace, and bring glad tidings of good things.
Their sound is gone out into all lands, and their words
unto the ends of the world."
— based on Romans 10:15, 18

It was Christmas in Bethlehem. Bethlehem, Pennsylvania. Putzes decorated the houses, and the Christmas stars had twenty-six points instead of five. On Christmas Eve, people ate food in the church services and lit candles with red paper frills on them.

It could have been last Christmas, or the Christmas before, or any Christmas all the way back to Christmas Eve of 1741 when Count Nikolaus von Zinzendorf of Germany visited America and helped his fellow Christians name their new village Bethlehem in honor of the baby Jesus. Zinzendorf was a nobleman who had allowed a small group of persecuted Christians from Moravia to settle on his estate in Germany. With Zinzendorf as their leader, these Christians, who came to be called "Moravians," soon sent missionaries all over the world. Some of these were the colonists who settled in Bethlehem. They brought Christmas customs with them that are still part of Christmas in modern Bethlehem and in Moravian congregations everywhere.

The Moravian star has many tips that point from its center in every direction. It shines with lights from within as it hangs in the church at Christmastime. Many Moravians build a *putz*, a nativity scene, in their homes. Besides the figures of Mary and Joseph and Jesus in the center of the putz, they often add other things such as farmhouses, castles, or sheep on a hillside. The Moravians say that their putzes "represent the world centered about the wondrous manger."[1] The highlight of a Moravian Christmas is a Christmas Eve "lovefeast," to mark God's love for mankind and Christians' love for each other. The lovefeasts are patterned after the practice of the first Christians who met to eat meals together.

At a Moravian lovefeast, worshipers sit in their pews and sing or listen to songs as men pass up and down the rows handing out mugs of milky coffee. Women give each person a sweet bun from big baskets. When all have been served, all eat together with thanksgiving and reverence. The Christmas service ends with each person holding high a lighted red-ruffed beeswax candle in the darkened church. The candles remind everyone that Jesus is the Light of the World. The flames encourage believers to let God's love burn in their hearts so that they might be Christ's faithful witnesses to a weary world.

That spirit of love and missionary enthusiasm was typical of the early Moravian church. Moravians were among the first Protestants to send out missionaries. They sent them throughout the world at a time when travel was difficult, and they sent them to peoples neglected and considered unimportant by many other Christians. And it all began with a love that burned in the heart of

a young teenage boy.

Count Nikolaus von Zinzendorf was born into wealth and privilege. His father died when he was a baby, and he was raised by his devout Christian grandmother. While a boy at boarding school in Halle, Germany, Zinzendorf and his friends formed a club they called the "Order of the Mustard Seed." The boys knew they were members of the nobility and that they would have money and power when they were grown. So they promised each other to use their influence to spread the gospel when they became men. Besides Zinzendorf, out of that little boy's club came a cardinal, a president, and an archbishop.

Zinzendorf grew up to give refuge and leadership to Moravians, who had been almost wiped out by religious persecution. In 1731 the grown-up Count Zinzendorf visited Denmark, where he met a slave from the West Indies who told him of the troubles of his people. Zinzendorf remembered his boyhood promise and returned home to Germany. There he found volunteers among the Moravians who went as missionaries to live among the slaves of Saint Thomas in the West Indies. Later, the Moravians sent others to preach the gospel of peace to Greenland, Africa, Tibet, Central America, Palestine, and Alaska. They ministered to slaves, refugees, and lepers with medicine, schools, and the glad tidings of good things — hope and salvation through Jesus Christ. Today, the great majority of Moravians live in those lands rather than Europe or the United States.

At heart, a Moravian Christmas is a mission-minded Christmas. And missions is at the heart of the Christmas story. Jesus came in love to save the world. His people go in love to tell this good news everywhere. The last words that Jesus spoke to His disciples were, "You will be my witnesses . . . to the ends of the earth."

NOTE

1. Adelaide L. Fries, *Customs and Practices of the Moravian Church* (Winston-Salem, N.C.: Board of Christian Education and Evangelism of the Moravian Church, 1973), 43. This book is a key source for their history and Christmas customs.

Part of the text of this entry is accompanied by track 22 on the CD.

Did the Mouse Do It?

*"Why do the nations so furiously rage together? and why
do the people imagine a vain thing? The kings of the
Earth rise up, and the rulers take counsel together
against the Lord and against His anointed."*
— based on Psalm 2:1-2

Was it the mouse that nibbled on the airways of the organ — that caused the organ to break — that caused the priest to worry about the music at his Christmas service — that inspired the creation of a simple little song that could be sung without an organ — that gave us that favorite of carols: "Silent Night"? Probably not.

Like many other legends of popular culture, the story behind the creation of "Silent Night" is a mixture of truth, mistaken facts, and romantic tales. And sometimes the truth, as is always said, is stranger than the fiction. Isn't it surprising that the very first time "Silent Night" was ever sung, it was in a peaceful, snow-covered village church in Austria? It was a church named, of all names, for St. Nicholas himself. Franz Gruber, the organist at St. Nicholas-in-Oberndorf, told the story of that first performance.

> On 24 December 1818 Herr Joseph Mohr . . . brought a poem to the organist Franz Gruber . . . asking him to set it for two solo voices, choir and guitar accompaniment. Gruber fulfilled this request on the same evening with a simple and easy composition, which was performed immediately afterwards and with some success on that same holy night.

Joseph Mohr was the new priest at the little chapel in Oberndorf, Austria, that Christmas Eve of 1818. He and his village choir typically might prepare a fine concert for the midnight Christmas mass. But this year, the organ had broken down. Perhaps it *was* a snacking mouse. Maybe it was only pipes rusted from the moist air of the river town. Or possibly it was something else.

In any case, Father Mohr had written a simple poem with six verses and asked his organist, Franz Gruber, to compose a tune that they could sing together to the accompaniment of Father Mohr's guitar. Herr Gruber, who was an accomplished composer, wrote the music that Christmas Eve of 1818. But it was many years before the world gave the credit for their lovely carol of peace to these two humble musicians.

Like a fire brigade handing off a bucket of water from hand to hand, the words and music for "Silent Night" were passed from place to place, changing along the way, until its source was completely forgotten. By the time the carol became popular in the United States, most people thought it was an anonymous German folk song. Franz Gruber helped to prove his and Mohr's authorship when a Berlin-based committee investigated the origins of "Silent Night" in 1854.

The village of Oberndorf heard "Silent Night" for the first time because their organ was broken. The world heard "Silent Night" because of the master organ builder who finally came to repair that organ. When he returned to his

The keyboard of the organ presented by Handel to the Chapel of the Foundling Hospital, London

home in the Tyrol region of Western Austria, he took with him a copy of the song. It was heard there by the Strassers, a family of glove-making folksingers. They called it "The Song from Heaven" and sang it to attract business as they sold their gloves at the German trade fairs. Their version, which differed some-what from Mohr's and Gruber's, was published in Dresden and became popular in Europe. Another Tyrolean family, the singing Rainers, brought "Silent Night" to the United States, just as if they were an early version of the "Sound of Music" clan.

"Silent night. . . . All is calm. . . . Sleep in heavenly peace."

From its opening refrain and the unforgettable conclusion of its first verse to the sweetness of its melody, "Silent Night" is a song of peace. It is the ideal Christmas song. Christmas is supposed to be about peace. Jesus is "the Prince of Peace," after all. The Jews of Jesus' time, like us, hoped for a Messiah who would save them from their enemies and bring earthly peace and prosperity.

Peace on earth of that sort didn't happen then, and it hasn't happened yet. There have always been those who hate God. There has always been warfare between good and evil. Jesus once said, "I did not come to bring peace, but a sword" (Matthew 10:34). Jesus inspires rage from those who hate God's law. He is not a God who can be ignored. King Herod tried to destroy Jesus at His birth. Pilate arranged His death. Yet even though God's enemies succeed for a time, the promise is that God is in control. His enemies are always doomed to fail. King Herod could not kill baby Jesus. Pilate could not keep Him in His grave. With His resurrection, Jesus conquered death and provided a way for us to have peace with God. And one day, when Jesus comes again to judge the world, evil and evildoers will be finally and everlastingly defeated. On that day, there will come the peace on earth that everyone hopes for.

Until then, God's people can "sleep in heavenly peace," knowing that our Father is watching over us and that He will not fail.

This entry is accompanied by track 23 on the CD.

Out on Highway 50

"I know that my Redeemer liveth, and that He shall stand at the latter day upon the earth: And though worms destroy this body, yet in my flesh shall I see God. For now is Christ risen from the dead, the first-fruits of them that sleep."
— based on Job 19:25-26; 1 Corinthians 15:20

Around Delta, in western Colorado, almost everyone knows about the Christmas tree. That's all it's called too. Just plain "the Christmas tree." It's out on Highway 50 about fifteen miles from Delta, on the road to Grand Junction. Travelers on that road can't miss the tree. It's the only one in sight. In fact, it's about the only thing to see on that stretch of road. The two-lane highway winds up and down through hills and gullies, through a landscape that looks almost like a desert. Nothing much grows out there. The dirt isn't any good for nurturing living things, and the wind blows hard. There are no people. No buildings. Only some scraggly, weedy, yellowish grass — and the Christmas tree.

The original tree was a fifteen-foot evergreen, a juniper, fat and nicely shaped, just like a Christmas tree should be. It stood so close to the side of the road that someone driving by in a car could stick out a hand and come near to touching it. The tree leaned toward the highway, almost seeming to reach for such a touch.

Decorating the tree for Christmas each year is nothing planned, nothing fancy. Motorists stop to add a decoration here and there. The tree shows off bits of tinsel and mismatched garland strands. In years past, the tree has worn just about every kind of trim. Once someone left a tree-shaped car air freshener. Others have decorated it with crayon-colored paper plates, bows, fruit, and store-bought ornaments. One lady left a little note, "The good news, God sent his son." No one knows how the Christmas tree got there or how it survived in that barren land for nearly thirty years.

Finally, around 1989, it died. Maybe it was the two bitter cold snaps after a mild fall that killed it. Maybe it was just too much attention. The townspeople planted a new evergreen. It wouldn't have quite been Christmas otherwise, without the tree there, in its glory by the side of the road. The decorating tradition continues, as it has for so many years.

A traveling writer once called the tree out on Highway 50 "a kind of miracle."

And, surviving as it did where nothing else of any account grows, it certainly does seem a miracle. But for thousands of years, that is what the green trees of winter have always reminded people of — the miracle of life.

Whether it's green growth in the forsaken landscape along Highway 50; forests of evergreen trees in the white snow; laurel bushes on the mountain slopes; winter's red berries among the green holly; the firs and cedars, spruces and pines we can decorate in December because they did not shed their needles when the oak and maple and birch dropped red and yellow leaves; or even the woody winter branches that seem dead but can be brought indoors to bud — all seem like miracles.

Pagans and Christians alike have paid attention to the meaning represented in the evergreen trees and in the plants that live when all else seems dead. The snow is like the cold and hard touch of death. But, in winter, evergreens are the evidence of life. In past times, warmth was not so easily had, and life was not so easy to hang on to. In such times, greenery and blooms in winter were a cause for celebration and wonder. Winter life was honored by many different cultures and religions. Many pagan religions had superstitious beliefs of a life-giving power in evergreens.

It's not surprising that trees and green things should cause people to wonder and look beyond themselves. In the first chapter of the New Testament book of Romans, the apostle Paul tells us that from the works of creation all of humanity can see the evidence of God. God "has made [Himself] plain to them . . . from what [He has] made, so that men are without excuse" (Romans 1:19-20). It is God who is the giver of life. He is the reason that trees are green in winter, that leafless branches bud and bloom and that we, ourselves, "live and move and have our being" (Acts 17:28).

God's power is not just made plain through what He has made. It was also made plain through death: Christ's death and His resurrection. Jesus Christ rose from the grave. That was the proof that He has power over death and the power to give us everlasting life. Even after death destroys us, God can make us new again. This is the promise for those who believe on the Lord Jesus Christ. They will be like a green tree in winter. They will be like a dead branch that blossoms. They shall live.

This entry is accompanied by track 24 on the CD.

Easter at Christmas

"Worthy is the Lamb that was slain, and hath redeemed us to God by His blood, to receive power, and riches, and wisdom, and strength, and honour, and glory, and blessing. Blessing, and honour, glory, and power, be unto Him that sitteth upon the throne, and unto the Lamb, for ever and ever. Amen."
— based on Revelation 5:12, 9, 13

Look at the lamb. Look at the lamb. Look at the blood of the lamb on the doorposts. The destroying angel saw the lamb's blood on the doors of the homes of the people of Israel, and they were saved. This happened in the time of Moses when God's people were slaves in the land of Egypt. God had seen the misery and suffering of His people and had given them Moses to rescue them from their slavery. Moses was going to lead them to a good land of their own.

Pharaoh, the lord of Egypt, did not want to lose his slaves. "I will not let Israel go," he said. Who else would build his great monuments? So the Lord God sent a judgment upon Pharaoh and the people of Egypt. God caused the River Nile to stink with the smell of blood, and He sent frogs and gnats and flies. He sent a disease to destroy their animals and boils to rot their skin, and He sent hail and locusts and darkness. In these plagues, God made a distinction between His people, whom He protected, and their enemies, the Egyptians. God did these things so that Egypt would know that there was a true God and so that Israel would know that they could be saved only by God's mighty hand.

Even then, Pharaoh would not let the Israelites leave his land. So it was that the last and most terrible of plagues came upon the people of Egypt. The warning was given to the Israelites and to all those who followed the way of the Lord God, that they were to kill a year-old male lamb. It had to be a perfect lamb.

With the blood of this lamb, they painted the sides and tops of their doors. Wherever there was a household whose doors were covered by the blood, those inside would be saved. At midnight, the angel of the Lord passed over the land of Egypt. In every home of the Egyptians where there was no blood on the door, the angel killed the firstborn child of the family. No home among the Egyptians was left untouched, from the palace of Pharaoh, to the ugliest hut of the lowest servant.

By this awful destruction, the people of Israel were delivered from their slavery. Pharaoh sent them out of his land. It was the evil and sin of Pharaoh that brought death to Egypt. But it was not by their own goodness that Moses and the Israelites were saved. It was the blood of the lambs that saved them. The blood was not magic. It was God's sign that sin is deadly and that a sacrifice is required to make things right.

Salvation came only through God. Ever after that first Passover, the people of Israel remembered the blood of the lamb with a yearly ceremony. It was a reminder of their need for salvation and their need for a savior. Long after the days of Pharaoh and Moses, the prophet Isaiah spoke of another lamb, the Messiah, who would be a sacrifice and a Savior for the whole world. The Messiah would provide salvation not from slavery, but from sin.

The Christmas story tells of the arrival of this Messiah who is also called the Lamb of God. The meaning of His name, "Lamb of God," is part of the Easter story. This story of salvation begins with the birth of Jesus. At the first Christmas the angels and the prophets spoke of the salvation that Jesus would bring.

An angel told Joseph, "He will save his people from their sins." An angel told the shepherds, "A Savior has been born to you." Zechariah prophesied that Jesus would bring His people "salvation through the forgiveness of their sins." Simeon held the baby Jesus and thanked God, saying, "My eyes have seen your salvation." And John the Baptist, the messenger of the Messiah, cried out when he saw Jesus coming to him, "Look, the Lamb of God, who takes away the sin of the world!"

God's justice requires that sin be punished by death. Even we know that it would be terribly wrong if there were no justice, no punishment for sin, no penalty for evil. God cannot allow that to happen. But God's love provides an escape: He paid the death penalty Himself. Jesus took the punishment for the sins of the whole world when He died on the cross. Easter is the reason for Christmas. Jesus was born so that He could die for us. He is the Lamb of God whose death and resurrection bring life to sinners.

Look at the Lamb. Worthy is the Lamb. Where else can we go to lose our sins except to Jesus, the Messiah, the precious Lamb of God.

This entry is accompanied by track 25 on the CD.

Why the King Stood Up

*"Hallelujah! For the Lord God Omnipotent reigneth. The
kingdom of this world is become the kingdom of our
Lord and of His Christ; and He shall reign for ever and
ever, King of Kings, and Lord of Lords. Hallelujah!"*
— based on Revelation 19:6; 11:15; 19:16

They stand up for *Messiah*. Whether it's a *Messiah* performed by profes-
sionals at a major concert hall or a *Messiah* sing-along in a local church,
when the choir begins to sing the "Hallelujah Chorus," concert-goers
rise to their feet. The standing tradition supposedly began with King George at
the first London performance of *Messiah* in 1743. The story has several versions.

One early historian heard it secondhand that George II and the entire audi-
ence "started up" when they heard the beautiful line, "For the Lord God
Omnipotent reigneth." Others claim that the king (who was a great fan of
Handel's) stood first. Naturally, if the king rises, everyone else has to stand
with him. Another story has it that the king was just arriving in the music hall
as the "Hallelujah Chorus" began, and everyone stood to welcome him.

However it started, the custom of standing was the fashion in Handel's lifetime and remains popular today. Those early audiences were impressed with
more than just the music of *Messiah*. They understood the story it told of a
Savior. They stood up to honor the Son of God. The story was so important to
them that many did not want to go to a show about the Messiah. They thought
that such music should be heard only in a church. Some in London worried that
the story of Messiah was too serious a subject for mere "Diversion and
Amusement." One critic wrote a letter to the newspaper complaining that the
theater was an unfit place for a religious performance and that the popular
singers of the day were too worldly to sing such songs. Handel even changed
the name of his oratorio for its first performance in London. He advertised it as
A New Sacred Oratorio. Handel may have thought that Londoners wouldn't
like to hear the name of Messiah associated with playhouses that also offered
Italian operas and love stories.

Nowadays we may think that such opinions are old-fashioned and strange.
But those old ideas are good reminders of God's majesty and power. Charles
Jennens, the man who arranged the words of *Messiah* for Handel, knew that
he was telling the most excellent of all stories. He wrote a letter to his friend

"I know that my Redeemer liveth" – *heavenly choirs of angels echo these words*

saying he hoped Handel's music would be good enough to accompany the words from the Bible. This is what Jennens wrote about *Messiah:* "I hope [Handel] will lay out his whole Genius and Skill upon it, that the Composition may excell all his former Compositions, as the Subject excells every other Subject. The Subject is Messiah."

Jennens's arrangement calls attention to the excellence of *Messiah* in the solo that comes right after the "Hallelujah Chorus." It begins, "I know that my Redeemer liveth." Jesus, the Messiah, is excellent because He is our Redeemer, the One who rescues us, saves us, ransoms us, and sets us free from sin. He is the One whom George Frideric Handel called "my sweet Lord and Savior" as he lay dying. Charles Jennens chose his Hallelujah words from the nineteenth chapter of the book of Revelation, the last book of the Bible. It is a book of hope for God's people with its promise that sin will be judged and evil defeated. The heavenly scene in Revelation 19 is of a huge crowd of people gathered to sing praises to God. Four times they shout "Hallelujah!" with voices that are "like the roar of rushing waters and like loud peals of thunder" (Revelation 19:6). With their hallelujahs, they cry out: "Let us rejoice and be glad and give [God] glory!" (v. 7).

This is Christmas Eve. This is the night for us to join with the heavenly host: Rejoice that the kingdom of this world, with all its sorrow and trouble, will one day become the kingdom of our Lord. Be glad for the Bethlehem promise of hope and peace. Give God the glory for sending us Jesus, the Redeemer and Savior of our souls.

This is Christmas Eve. This is the night to honor the Holy Christ Child who is King of kings and Lord of lords. We may stand up for fine music and special occasions, but Jesus is worthy of much more. The Son of God has come among us. "Who can stand" before Him . . . ? (Malachi 3:2). Before Him, "every knee [must] bow and every tongue confess that Jesus Christ is Lord" (Philippians 2:10-11) This is Christmas Eve. This is the night of all nights to thank Messiah. The baby of Bethlehem is our mighty God. He offers the gift of salvation to any who will accept it. Let us bow our heads, bend our knees, and rejoice.

This entry is accompanied by track 26 on the CD.

The original edition of Messiah *by George Frideric Handel,*
in a red leather cover with embossed gold decoration.

Read More About It

First Week in Advent: Sunday
Why the Gentlemen Couldn't Wear Swords

Details, Details
- Handel started out his life as Georg Friedrich Händel. He changed his German-spelled name to an English spelling later, signing his letters as "George Frideric Handel."
- Handel called his oratorio *Messiah*, not THE *Messiah*.

Meanings
- An oratorio is a musical rendition, usually of a biblical subject. With chorus, soloists, orchestra, and story line, an oratorio has the dramatic appeal of an opera but without the acting.
- Libretto comes from the Italian word for book. The libretto is the words that accompany the music of an opera or an oratorio. Often the libretto is called a "wordbook" when it is sold at public performances.

Dig Deeper
- Listen to *Messiah*. Look for alternate versions at your library or music store. One example of an alternate version is *Handel's Messiah, A Soulful Celebration*. This vibrant interpretation uses a variety of styles from black culture.
- Attend a concert or try singing *Messiah* yourself. Many communities have "*Messiah* Sing-Alongs" at Christmas.

First Week in Advent: Monday
Secret of the Desert Caves

Details, Details
- The Bible readings for this story and the next one are the first and second halves of the preface that Charles Jennens wrote for *Messiah*. It is never sung.
- The Dead Sea Scrolls date from about three hundred years before Christ to A.D 68 when the Qumran community was destroyed by the Roman army.
- The seven original scrolls from cave 1 are displayed in the Shrine of the Book in Jerusalem. This magnificent building is half-buried to commemorate that the scrolls were hidden for centuries. The roof of the building is in the shape of one of the lids of the jars that held the scrolls.
- For more than forty years, a small group of scholars kept exclusive control of the scrolls, much to the dismay of others who had an interest in them. In 1991, the Huntington Library of California released photographic copies of the scrolls against the wishes of the controlling group. This release has resulted in increased study and interest in the scrolls.

Meanings
- Messiah means "anointed one," from the Hebrew word *mashiah*. The word relates to the Old Testament practice of marking someone as priest or king by the ceremony of anointing – pouring oil on the head (see 1 Samuel 16:1-13). The Old Testament looked forward to the coming of God's promised Messiah – the Savior of Israel.
- The word *Christ* is a direct Greek translation of the Hebrew word *mashiah* ("messiah" or "anointed one").

Find It in the Bible
- Isaiah 7:14; 9:6-7; 53:5; Micah 5:2 – The promised Messiah.
- John 20:31 – Jesus is "the Christ."
- Colossians 1:25-26 – The mystery of the ages revealed.

First Week in Advent: Tuesday
Finding the Perfect Gift

Details, Details
- O. Henry (1862-1910) once said, "There are stories in everything." He published hundreds of short stories in magazines and book collections. He is famous for his use of the surprise ending. Two other Christmas tales, *Whistling Dick's Christmas Stocking* (his first published story) and *Christmas by Injunction* are typical of O. Henry's humorous, casual style.

Find it in the Bible
- Proverbs, chapters 1-4 – Wisdom.
- Matthew 6:19-21 – Where your treasure is.

Dig Deeper
- Read the original version of *The Gift of the Magi* by O. Henry. It was first published in a 1906 book of short stories entitled *The Four Million*. It is now widely available in various anthologies, including *The Book of Virtues* by William J. Bennett.

First Week in Advent: Wednesday
Christmas Truce

Details, Details
- World War I began with the assassination of Archduke Ferdinand of Austria in June 1914.
- On December 25, 1914, some of the one thousand muddy Belgian soldiers who had camped out in the Church of St. Nicholas in Furnes, Belgium, knelt around an altar to celebrate Christmas.

Meanings
- Iniquity is sin. Sin is what separates us from God and puts us at war with Him.

Find It in the Bible
- Romans, chapter 5 – How to obtain pardon and peace through Jesus Christ.

Dig Deeper
- Read "In Flanders Field," a popular poem from World War I by John McCrae.

First Week in Advent: Thursday
The Messenger

Details, Details
- Jews who still await the Messiah await also the arrival of the messenger Elijah. As part of the Passover ceremony, it is traditional to leave an empty cup and place setting at the table for Elijah. At the end of the meal, children of the household open the door to look for Elijah.
- There were twenty-four priestly families in Israel, all descendants of Aaron, the brother of Moses. Zechariah was from the family of Abijah, the eighth in the order of priests.
- John's mother, Elizabeth, was a relative of Mary, the mother of Jesus.

Meanings
- Zechariah's song of praise in Luke 1:67-79 is traditionally called the Benedictus from the Latin word meaning "praise be."
- Repentance, in the words of the *Book of Common Prayer*, is to be "heartily sorry for these our misdoings." Repentance is a change of heart and mind, a turning away from sin and a turning toward (seeking) God.
- A prophet is one who delivers God's message.

Find It in the Bible
- 2 Kings 2:11-12 – Elijah taken up into heaven.
- Malachi 3:1; 4:5-6 – Malachi's prophecies about John.
- Luke 1:5-23 – John's birth.
- Matthew 3:3; Mark 1:2-5; Luke 3:4-6; John 1:23 – John fulfills Isaiah's prophecy.
- Matthew 11:10; Mark 1:2; Luke 7:27 – John fulfills Malachi's prophecy.
- Matthew 11:14; Mark 9:12; Luke 1:17 – John's ministry was in the spirit of Elijah.

First Week in Advent: Friday
Star of Wonder

Details, Details
- Johannes Kepler (1571-1630), the famous German mathematician, published a book in which he calculated the date of Christ's birth and discussed the theory that the Star of Bethlehem was a conjunction (the coming close together) of planets.
- No one knows why the Magi associated the "star" they saw with the birth of a king of the Jews. Some have suggested that the wise men gave special meaning

to the unusual triple meeting of Jupiter and Saturn that took place around the time of Christ's birth. Astrologers of that time identified the planet Jupiter with kings and the planet Saturn with the Jews. The conjunction of these planets would have been associated with important events.
- An early Church Father, Augustine (A.D. 354-430), wrote that at Christ's birth, "a star which had not hitherto existed arose."

Find It in the Bible
- Romans 8:18-24 – The new creation.

Dig Deeper
- Find detailed information on theories of the Bethlehem star in *The Star of Bethlehem: An Astronomer's Confirmation* by David Hughs (New York: Walker and Company, 1979). Much of the information in this chapter comes from this book.

First Week in Advent: Saturday
The Legend of the Flying Snakes

Details, Details
- The location of "The Lost City" of Ubar was discovered in the early 1990s after archaeologists teamed up with the National Aeronautics Space Administration (NASA). They used pictures from satellites in space to find the old caravan routes that were hidden under the sand. You can read more about it at NASA's "Observatorium" Website (http://observe.ivv.nasa.gov/nasa/exhibits/ubar/ubar_1.html).

Meanings
- *Lord of Hosts* is one of the names of God. It indicates His power. It suggests God's holy army, His lordship, and His direction of all created beings and powers.
- Incense is a material that smokes and has a pleasant smell when it burns. In Latin, *incendere* means "to set on fire."

Find It in the Bible
- Exodus 30:34-38 – Directions for making and using the holy incense.

Dig Deeper
- Check out *Arabia's Frankincense Trail* by Thomas J. Abercrombie in your library's back issues of *National Geographic* (October 1985). It includes photographs of frankincense trees.

Second Week in Advent: Sunday
Why?

Details, Details
- In earlier centuries, the number of children massacred by Herod was exaggerated to

be as high as 3,000 to 144,000. Historians agree that only about six to twenty-five children were killed. This low number may explain why no historical record of the slaughter exists, except for the Bible's account. Herod's atrocities were so numerous that, for the writers of that time, the deaths of a few peasant children were probably not worth mentioning.
• Herod the Great rebuilt Solomon's temple for the Jews. All that remains of it today is the great "Wailing Wall" in Jerusalem.

Meanings
• Herod's murder of the Bethlehem boys is often called "The Slaughter of the Innocents." Some churches mark this event on December 28, Holy Innocents' Day. In some cultures, this day is celebrated much like Halloween with masks and costumes.
• Herod is not an individual name, but a family name. Herod the Great was the first of the Herodian dynasty that ruled for four generations in Judea. Herod Antipas had John the Baptist beheaded and also questioned Jesus at Pilate's request. Herod Agrippa I put the apostle Peter in prison where he was released by an angel. The apostle Paul made his defense before Herod Agrippa II.

Find It in the Bible
• Matthew, chapter 2 – Herod the Great, the Magi, and the children.

Dig Deeper
• Robert Green's children's book *Herod the Great* (New York: Little, Franklin Watts, 1996) is a good introduction to this subject.

Second Week in Advent: Monday
The Fire's Work

Details, Details
• In Iraq, archaeologists excavating the royal tombs of ancient Ur (3000-2000 B.C.) discovered a helmet that had been beaten and formed from a single nugget of gold.

Meanings
• Sons of Levi. The Levites were a tribe of Israel who served as priestly assistants. In the book of Malachi, they represent those who should be faithful servants of the Lord.
• Refining is the process of purifying metals by heat. Impurities are skimmed off after they separate from the melted metal. Refined gold or silver is the most valuable.
• Solomon was king of Israel almost one thousand years before Christ. He reigned during Israel's golden age — golden because of Solomon's wisdom and his wealth. His father, King David, planned and collected materials for the great temple of the Lord that Solomon built.

Find It in the Bible
- 1 Kings, chapter 10 – Solomon's wisdom and splendor.

Dig Deeper
- Facts about gold and its history can be found at The Gold Institute's Website (www.goldinstitute.org).

Second Week in Advent: Tuesday
Daughter of Her Son

Details, Details
- Spectators waited in line to view Michelangelo's Pietà from moving walkways at the 1964 New York World's Fair. The Pietà had never before left Rome.
- Michelangelo inscribed his name and the comment that he had "made this" on Mary's sash. It was the only time he ever signed his artwork.
- Michelangelo carved two more Pietàs. He was dissatisfied with one and broke part of it. Michelangelo was working on his third Pietà only a few days before he died. In 1998 art experts arranged for IBM scientists to make a three-dimensional computer model of the original. Containing nearly two billion bits of data, the model is the most detailed ever made of a piece of art.

Meanings
- *Madonna* is an Italian word meaning "my lady."
- *Incarnation* is a theological term meaning that God became human — that Jesus is both God and man. The word comes from the Latin for "taking flesh."

Find It in the Bible
- John 1:1-4, 14 – Jesus, the "Word," is God.
- Hebrews 4:15–16 – Jesus understands our weaknesses.

Dig Deeper
- Take time to visit a museum and view its Madonna and Child artworks.
- Robin Richmond's children's book, *Introducing Michelangelo* (Little, Brown and Company, Boston, 1991), includes fine photographs of Michelangelo's three Pietàs.

Second Week in Advent: Wednesday
No Christmas Allowed!

Details, Details
- The Pilgrims arrived in Plymouth during December of 1620 and spent Christmas building their first houses. The next Christmas, some of the company told Governor William Bradford that it was against their conscience to work on Christmas Day. He told them that "if they made it a mater of conscience, he would spare them till they were better informed." But when he came home for lunch with the men who had been working, he found the others playing sports

in the street rather than keeping to their houses and devotions. "So he went to them and tooke away their implements, and told them it was against his conscience that they should play, and others worke."

Meanings
- Puritans were sixteenth-century Protestants who wanted to purify and reform the Church of England. One group of Puritans actually separated from the Church of England. These "Separatists" established the Plymouth colony in New England. They came to be called the Pilgrims because of their religious quest. Other Puritans stayed within the church to reform it. Some of these wealthier Puritans formed the Massachusetts Bay Company and settled near Boston.

Find It in the Bible
- Matthew 5:14-16 – "City on a hill."

Dig Deeper
- *The Battle for Christmas* by Stephen Nissenbaum (New York: Alfred A. Knopf, 1996) is a good cultural history of the celebration of Christmas in the United States.

Second Week in Advent: Thursday
Who Were They?

Details, Details
- Persians invading Bethlehem in A.D. 614 are said to have spared the Church of the Nativity because its mosaic of the wise men showed them wearing Persian clothes.
- Traditionally the gifts of the Magi are seen to represent Jesus as King (gold), God (frankincense), and Savior (myrrh).

Meanings
- *Magi* (singular, *magus*) comes from an old Persian word, *magu*. It has an uncertain original meaning. Magi were first mentioned by the ancient Greek historian, Herodotus, as a tribe of Medes with priestly functions. The term came to apply to astrologers, wise men, and magicians.
- Epiphany is a celebration on January 6 to mark the visit of the Magi to worship Jesus. It represents the revelation of Jesus as Savior of the world.

Find It in the Bible
- Matthew 7:7-8; Hebrew 11:6 – Seeking and finding.

Dig Deeper
- Read more about the Magi and the star in Paul L. Maier's book *In the Fullness of Time: A Historian Looks at Christmas, Easter, and the Early Church* (Grand Rapids: Kregel,1997).

Second Week in Advent: Friday
Light

Details, Details
- Before Thomas Edison invented the lightbulb, families mounted candles on their trees on Christmas Eve and stood water buckets nearby in case of a fire. In the Middle Ages people put candles in their windows to "guide the Christ child on His way," or lit one giant candle to burn for the twelve days of Christmas.
- Advent wreaths usually include three purple candles to represent Christ as king, and one pink or rose candle to represent hope and joy. Advent begins with the lighting of the first of the purple candles on the fourth Sunday before Christmas. The pink candle is lit during the last week of Advent. These candles are often replaced for the twelve days of Christmas with one white "Christ candle." The green wreath is an ancient symbol of victory.
- Galileo was the first person to try to measure the speed of light.
- Special machines called cyclotrons can accelerate atomic particles to speeds near the speed of light.

Find it in the Bible
- James 1:17 – The Father of lights.
- Matthew 5:14-16; 2 Corinthians 3:13-18 – Reflections of the light.

Dig Deeper
- The children's section of a public library should have a number of books on light. They will be found with call numbers of 535.

Second Week in Advent: Saturday
She Wrapped Him in Swaddling Clothes

Details, Details
- The angel gave the shepherds a sign that would help them find the newborn Jesus: He would be wrapped in swaddling clothes (Luke 2:12).
- Modern research has confirmed that swaddling calms babies. Even Doctor Spock recommended it!
- The Japanese wrapped their babies upright in a basket called an *ejiko*. The Saami (Laplanders) wrap their babies in canoe-like containers that they carry on their backs while they tend the reindeer. Navajos wrap their children on cradleboards for carrying them.

Meanings
- Swathe also means to wrap in bandages and is an old-fashioned word for swaddle.

Find It in the Bible
- Ezekiel 16:4-5 – The unloved child.

Dig Deeper
- Visit an art museum and look for pictures of swaddled babies.

Third Week in Advent: Sunday
Christmas Angels

Details, Details
- In Bible times, two groups of Jewish leaders disagreed about the reality of angels. The Sadducees said that angels did not exist. The Pharisees said that they did (Acts 23:8).
- The Bible names only the angels Michael and Gabriel. But throughout history, others have invented names and jobs for many others. The apocryphal *Book of Tobit* includes a story about an archangel named Raphael.
- When God drove Adam and Eve from the Garden of Eden, He placed cherubim with flaming swords at the entrance to prevent them from touching the Tree of Life (Genesis 3:23-24).

Meanings
- The Hebrew *(malak)* and Greek *(aggelos)* words for angel both mean "messenger."

Find It in the Bible
- Isaiah 6:2-3 – The Bible's only description of seraphim.
- Ezekiel 1 and 10 – Ezekiel's visions of cherubim.
- Daniel 10:4-10 – Daniel's vision of an angel.
- Psalm 34:7; 91:11; Matthew 18:10; Hebrews 1:14 – Guardian angels.

Dig Deeper
- Billy Graham's best-seller entitled *Angels* was first published in 1975 and is now available in paperback (Dallas: Word Publishers, 1995).

Third Week in Advent: Monday
The Christmas Day Mystery

Details, Details
- There is no year zero in the B.C./A.D. calendar system that we use today.
- The Twelve Days of Christmas are the days between December 25 and Epiphany on January 6. Epiphany is sometimes called Twelfth Day, and it is the day that marks the visit of the Magi to Jesus.
- In 1752, England adopted the Gregorian calendar that we use today to replace Julius Caesar's old "Julian Calendar." The switch meant that the calendar was moved several days back. Thus January 6 became December 25. There were riots in parts of England when this change took place. People shouted, "Give us back our eleven days!" Even now, January 6 is sometimes called "Old Christmas."

Meanings
- Christmas is a combination of Christ + mass (a "festival of Christ"). The word was in use by A.D. 1050.
- In the gospel of Luke the shepherds are told they will find Jesus in the City of David (some Bible translations say "town of David"). This is Bethlehem, the hometown of David, Israel's greatest king. In the Old Testament, the phrase "City of David" always means Jerusalem, the capital city of Israel that was founded by King David.

Find It in the Bible
- 2 Corinthians 6:2 – Now is the day of salvation.

Third Week in Advent: Tuesday
The Carol Quiz

Details, Details
- Answers to the "Carol Quiz:" "Rejoice! Rejoice! Emmanuel shall come to thee" (*O Come, O Come, Emmanuel*); "This, this is Christ the King" (*What Child Is This?*); "Glory to the newborn King" (*Hark! The Herald Angels Sing*); "Peace on earth, good will to men" (*I Heard the Bells on Christmas Day*); "Jesus, He is born" (*The Huron Carol*); "O tidings of comfort and joy" (*God Rest Ye Merry, Gentlemen*).
- Jean de Brebeuf and other Jesuits left a remarkable series of journals that were reports of their missionary work in Huronia (the Huron lands near Quebec). Called "The Jesuit Relations" and "The Huron Relations," they are a fascinating eyewitness account of those times. Jean de Brebeuf was an outstanding example of a loving servant-missionary.

Meanings
- *Carol* comes from Greek *(choraulein)*, Latin *(choraula)*, and Old French *(caroler)* — words that all mean dancing in a circle.
- The Huron are also called the Wyandot Nation.
- Carolers who stroll the streets singing Christmas songs are called *waits* in Great Britain.

Find It in the Bible
- Psalm 100:1-2; Colossians 3:16 – Joyful songs.

Dig Deeper
- You can read about the history of the Huron people, missionary work by the Jesuits and the Methodists, "The Huron Carol," and the life and journals of Saint Jean de Brebeuf at the Wyandot Nation of Kansas Webpage (http://sfo.com/~denglish/wynaks/wyandot2.html).

Third Week in Advent: Wednesday
These Tired Eyes, These Wrinkled Hands

Details, Details
- Three ceremonies are required by Old Testament law after the birth of a boy. He must be circumcised at eight days. If he is a firstborn son, he must be redeemed at one month with five shekels of silver. When any son is forty days old (eighty days for a daughter), the mother must bring offerings for her purification — a year-old lamb (or pigeon or dove if she is poor) for a burnt offering and a pigeon or dove for a sin offering. Mary and Joseph fulfilled all of these requirements (Luke 2:21-24).
- As a reminder that God brought Israel out of slavery in Egypt, every firstborn Jewish male is considered dedicated to God's service (Exodus 13:14-16). The priestly tribe of Levi was set apart to serve in the temple in place of the firstborn. Even so, the "Redemption of the Firstborn" with five pieces of money was required and is still practiced today.
- Legend has it that Simeon was the son of Hillel and the father of Gamaliel, both famous Jewish teachers and Pharisees.

Meanings
- Simeon's song of praise in Luke 2:29-32 is traditionally called the *Nunc Dimittis*. They are the Latin words from the phrase in verse 29, "Now *[nunc]* dismiss *[dimittis]* your servant in peace."
- Mary and Joseph did bring a sacrificial lamb to the temple on the day of Mary's purification. That lamb was Jesus, the Lamb of God (John 1:29). The sacrifice of animals had to be repeated over and over, but the sacrifice of Jesus on the cross was "once for all."

Find It in the Bible
- Luke 2:22-40 – Story of Simeon and Anna.
- Numbers 18:14-16 – Redemption of the firstborn.
- Leviticus 12:1-8 – Offering for purification after a child is born.
- Hebrews 10:1-10 – Jesus the "once for all" sacrifice.

Third Week in Advent: Thursday
The Shoepolish Boy

Details, Details
- Saint Augustine once wrote, "I have read in Plato and Cicero sayings that are very wise and very beautiful, but I never read in either of them: 'Come unto me all ye that labor and are heavy laden.'"
- Charles Dickens lived from 1812-1870.

Meanings
- *Hart* is an old-fashioned term for a male deer.
- *Dumb* is an old-fashioned word meaning unable to speak.

Find It in the Bible
- Matthew 15:29-31 – Jesus heals.

Dig Deeper
- Read *A Christmas Carol* (it is short, especially compared to Dickens's other novels) or watch a video version.

Third Week in Advent: Friday
They Fall Down and Can't Get Up Again

Details, Details
- A shepherd who wants to trim a sheep's hooves or shear its wool places the animal in "the shepherd's chair hold." The sheep will not move when it is in this sort of sitting position with its feet off the ground. It acts dazed, just as it would if it fell down. People who knew sheep would have known exactly what it meant when Jesus' silence before His accusers was compared to a sheep that is silent before the shearer (Isaiah 53:7; Acts 8:32). He didn't defend Himself when they accused Him.
- To get a mother sheep to nurse a lamb that is not her own, a shepherd may rub the new lamb with sweetened water for the ewe to lick or cover the orphan with the skin of the ewe's own lamb that died.
- The Jewish holiest of days, The Day of Atonement, is announced by blowing the trumpet-like "shofar," which is made from a ram's horn.

Meanings
- In Israel, a shepherd's reed flute is called a *zamoora*. The Hebrew word for psalm *(mizmor)* means "to play on a zamoora."

Find It in the Bible
- Luke 2:8-16 – Story of the shepherds and angels.
- Ezekiel 34:1-10 – The bad shepherd.
- Ezekiel 34:11-31 – The good shepherd.
- Psalm 23 – The Lord is our shepherd.

Dig Deeper
- Phillip Keller's books offer unusual insight into the meaning of "The Good Shepherd" (*A Shepherd Looks at Psalm 23* and *A Shepherd Looks at the Good Shepherd & His Sheep*, both by Moody Press, Chicago, 1970, 1978).
- A large public library should have a copy of John D. Whiting's article, *Among the Bethlehem Shepherds*, in the December 1926 edition of *National Geographic* (729-753). It includes excellent photographs of the shepherding life that has not changed since the time of Jesus.

Third Week in Advent: Saturday
The Reindeer People

Details, Details
- Reindeer are the only species of deer ever domesticated. Wild reindeer are commonly called "caribou."
- Reindeer are the only deer in which both males and females have antlers. The antlers are solid bone and are shed every year.

Meanings
- A yoke is a harness of wood or rope that a human or an animal wears to carry or pull a heavy load. The word is commonly used to symbolize slavery or servanthood.
- *Burthen* is the old spelling for burden, something (usually heavy) that is carried.
- *Laplanders* is a common term for the Scandinavian native peoples who live in several countries north of the Arctic Circle. They are preferably identified by their own name, the Saami, since the word Lapland is somewhat unkind, coming from a word that means "a patch of cloth for mending."

Dig Deeper
- Read about how Christian lost his burden of sin in John Bunyan's *Pilgrim's Progress*. A beautifully illustrated children's adaptation is entitled *Dangerous Journey* (Grand Rapids: Eerdmans, 1985).
- Hugh Beach chronicles his experiences with the Saami in *A Year in Lapland: Guest of the Reindeer Herders* (Washington, D.C.: Smithsonian Institution Press, 1993). (Most of the information from this chapter comes from this book. It tells a lot of details of Saami words and customs.)

Fourth Week in Advent: Sunday
Castle or Cave?

Details, Details
- The cave beneath the Church of the Nativity in Bethlehem is the traditional site of Christ's birth. Parts of the church were built by the Roman Emperor Constantine in A.D. 326. As early as A.D. 150, Justin Martyr wrote that Christ was born in a cave. The church also displays a stone manger. In Bible times, mangers were more likely to be cut from stone than made of wood.
- Saint Francis of Assisi set up the first nativity scene (using real people and animals) in Greccio, Italy, in 1223.
- In 1759, King Carlo left Naples to become king of Spain (Charles III).
- *Presepi* are an important part of Christmas celebrations in Italian homes and churches today. Shops display elaborate scenes carved from butter or made of pastry, pasta, bread dough, or fruit.

Meanings
- *Presepio* (plural, *presepi*) is an Italian word that comes from the Latin meaning "in front of the fence." English speakers say "nativity scene" or "crib." In French it is *crêche*, in German, *krippe*, and in Spanish, *nacimiento*.

Find It in the Bible
- Isaiah 1:3 – Cattle and donkeys knowing their owner.

Dig Deeper
- For adults, a lovely (and challenging) meditation on Christ's birth is *The God in the Cave* from G. K. Chesterton's classic book *The Everlasting Man*. (Chesterton is also the author of the *Father Brown* mystery series.)

Fourth Week in Advent: Monday
Perfume of the Pharaohs

Details, Details
- On the cross Jesus was offered wine mixed with myrrh (to lessen the pain), but He did not take it (Mark 15:23).
- In the fourteenth century before Christ, Queen Hatshepsut of Egypt organized a sailing expedition to Somaliland in Africa to search for myrrh and frankincense. The explorers brought back myrrh trees that the queen planted on the terraces in front of the temple of her god, Amon-Re.

Meanings
- A transgression is the breaking of a law or command. It comes from a Latin word meaning "step across," as in stepping over a boundary line to trespass. Transgression is another word for sin.
- Sheba or Saba was in the southwest tip of Arabia. The Sabeans were ideally located to trade in the myrrh, frankincense, gold, and precious stones of South Arabia and Africa. Their camel caravans brought these exports to Israel and the north.

Find it in the Bible
- Genesis 37:25 – Joseph sold to myrrh traders.
- 1 Kings 10:1-13 – The Queen of Sheba traded spices with King Solomon.
- Esther 2:12 – Queen Esther beautified herself with myrrh.
- 2 Chronicles 16:14 – King Asa was buried on a bed of spices and perfumes.
- John 19:39-40 – Nicodemus buried Jesus with myrrh.
- Acts 2:24 – Jesus conquered death.
- John 14:19b – Life through Jesus.

Fourth Week in Advent: Tuesday
Lovefeast

Details, Details
- The famous English preacher John Wesley was converted through the witness of Moravians he met aboard a ship to America.
- The Moravian lovefeasts are celebrated at different times throughout the year. In other countries this simple meal could be tea or juice and peanuts or a cookie,

rather than coffee and a sweet bun.

• The motto of the Moravian church is: "In essentials unity; in nonessentials liberty; and in all things love."

Meanings

• Moravians are also called by their original name, "Unitas Fratrum" or "Unity of Brethren." The Unitas Fratrum was founded by followers of John Hus, who was burned at the stake in 1415 for his Bible-based beliefs. In the following years, members were widely persecuted. They survived in secret until they reorganized under the leadership and support of Count Zinzendorf in the early 1700s.

Find It in the Bible

• John 3:16; Romans 10:9-13 – The missionary message.
• Mark 16:15; Romans 10:14-15 – The missionary call.

Dig Deeper

• Visit the restored Moravian village of Old Salem in Winston-Salem, North Carolina.
• Information about the Moravian Church can be found at their Website (www.moravian.org).
• Read biographies of some of the great missionaries. Examples: Saint Patrick, Adoniram Judson, C. T. Studd, William Carey, Hudson and Maria Taylor, Saddhu Sundar Singh, Amy Carmichael, the five missionaries martyred by Aucas.

Fourth Week in Advent: Wednesday
Did the Mouse Do It?

Details, Details

• "Silent Night" was translated into English for a Massachusetts Sunday school hymnal in 1876 by John F. Young. He used only verses one, six, and two of Joseph Mohr's original lyrics. Young's is the English version that is still sung today.
• On Christmas Eve, 1949, at the dividing line between North and South Korea, loudspeakers played "Silent Night" for the soldiers, instead of the usual propaganda of the Korean War.
• Bing Crosby probably increased the popularity of "Silent Night" in the United States after singing it in the 1945 movie *The Bells of St. Mary's*.

Find It in the Bible

• Acts 4:21-31 – Peter and John speak out against the raging nations.

Dig Deeper

• Margaret Hodge's book *Silent Night: The Song and Its Story* tells the story of "Silent Night" in pictures (Grand Rapids: Eerdmans, 1997).
• Check your library's adult and children's sections under call numbers 783.6 for the stories behind other Christmas carols.

Fourth Week in Advent: Thursday
Out on Highway 50

Details, Details
- Legend claims that Christmas trees began with Martin Luther, who supposedly brought a fir tree indoors for his children and decorated it with candles. But the first written mention of a Christmas tree comes a little later — from Strasburg, Germany, in 1605. Christmas trees were popular in Germany long before they were common elsewhere.
- Queen Victoria and Prince Albert made Christmas trees popular in England and the United States. In 1848, a drawing of the royal family's tree at Windsor Castle was printed in a London newspaper. Two years later it was published in America by *Godey's Lady Book*. After those pictures appeared, people wanted trees in their own homes.

Meanings
- Some Christians decorate a Jesse Tree during the Advent season. It is trimmed with symbols of Christ's birth. The name comes from a prophecy in Isaiah 11:1 that the Messiah will be born from the line of King David, son of Jesse. Jesus is the new branch that "will come up from the stump of Jesse."

Find It in the Bible
- 1 Corinthians 15:12-58 – The why and how of resurrection.

Fourth Week in Advent: Friday
Easter at Christmas

Details, Details
- Jesus celebrated the Passover with His disciples just before He was crucified (Matthew 26:17-30). This "Last Supper" is remembered by Christians in Holy Communion, as Jesus commanded (1 Corinthians 11:23-26).

Meanings
- Passover is a translation of the Hebrew word *Pesach*. Passover is one of the most important of Jewish festivals.It is an eight-day celebration that marks Israel's deliverance from slavery in Egypt when the angel of the Lord "passed over" the homes protected by the blood of the lamb.
- We use the adjective *Paschal* for things related to Easter. "Paschal" comes from similar words in French, Latin, and Greek. All come from the word *Pesach*.

Find It in the Bible
- Exodus, chapters 11, 12 – The first Passover.
- 1 Peter 1:18-21 – Christ, the Lamb.

Dig Deeper
- You can check back in earlier stories for information about Jesus as Messiah (First Week, Monday, pp. 17–19), Zechariah and John the Baptist (First Week, Thursday, pp. 26–28), or Simeon and Anna (Third Week, Wednesday, p. 68–71).

CHRISTMAS EVE
Why the King Stood Up

Details, Details
- Handel died on April 14, 1759, the day before Easter Sunday. He was buried in Westminster Abbey. Then 110 years later, the body of Charles Dickens was laid in the grave next to Handel's.

Meanings
- *Hallelujah* comes from two Hebrew words, *halal* (to praise), and *Yah* (short for "Yahweh," a holy name for God). The word, meaning "Praise the Lord," occurs in the Bible only in Psalms and in Revelation, chapter 19. Alleluia comes from the Greek or Latin version of hallelujah.

Find It in the Bible
- Philippians 2:10-11 – Every knee shall bow.

Dig Deeper
- For more information, read *The Messiah Book: The Life & Times of G. F. Handel's Greatest Hit* by Peter Jacobi (New York: St. Martin's Press, 1982).
- A very nice illustrated edition of the *Messiah* libretto is *Messiah: The Wordbook for the Oratorio* (New York: Willa Perlman Books, 1992). Timothy Botts has also done an attractive *Messiah* with the text in calligraphy (Wheaton, Ill.: Tyndale, 1991).

Picture Sources

p. 6   Terra-cotta Bust of George Frideric Handel, by Roubillac (1695-1762). © The Bridgeman Art Library.

p. 11   The original score of Handel's *Messiah*. © The Bridgeman Art Library.

p. 14   *Dining on the Terrace*, by Franz Christoph Janneck. © Fine Art Photographic Library Ltd.

p. 18   The caves at Qumran, © Jon Arnold.

p. 21   *The Adoration of the Wise Men*, by Rembrandt van Rijn, 1632. The Hermitage Museum, St Petersburg.

p. 24   *Gassed* (detail), by John Singer Sargent, 1919, The Imperial War Museum, London.

p. 27   *The Immersion of the Pilgrims in the River Jordan*, by David Roberts, c.1840.

p. 30   *Handel Playing the Organ* in the interior of Covent Garden Theatre, from Ackermann's Microcosm of London, © The Bridgeman Art Library.

p. 33   *The Nativity with the Three Magi* (detail), by Jerome Bosch, Prado Museum, Madrid.

p. 37   *The Massacre of the Innocents*, by Maerten van Cleve (1527-81). © The Bridgeman Art Library.

p. 40   *The Nativity with the Three Magi* (detail), by Jerome Bosch, Prado Museum, Madrid.

p. 43   *The Holy Family*, pen and brush drawing by Rembrandt (1606-69). London, British Museum.

p. 47   *Jerusalem the Golden*, by Samuel Lawson Booth (1836-1928). © Fine Art Photographic Library Ltd.

p. 50   *The Three Wise Men*, from The Norfolk Triptych, c. 1415-20, Museum Boymans-van Beuningen, Rotterdam.

p. 51   *The Holy Family*, from The Norfolk Triptych, c. 1415-20, Museum Boymans-van Beuningen, Rotterdam.

p. 53   *The Light of the World*, by Holman Hunt (1827-1910), St. Paul's Cathedral, London.

p. 56   *The Shepherds Worship the Child*, by Rembrandt (1606-69). © The National Gallery, London.

p. 59   *An Angel*, by John Merlhuish Strudwick (1849-1937). © Fine Art Photographic Library Ltd.

p. 63   The Shepherds Fields, near Bethlehem. © Jon Arnold.

p. 66   *Glad Tidings*, by William Spittle (1858-1917), © Fine Art

Photographic Library Ltd.

p. 69   *The Song of Simeon* by Rembrandt (1606-69). © Stockholm National Museum.

p. 72   *An Irish Emigrant Landing at Liverpool,* by Erskine Nicol (c. 1841). © Christopher Wood Gallery, London.

p. 76   *The Nativity,* by Giotto, (c. 1305), Scrovegni Chapel, Padua. © Sacla, Florence.

p. 79   *Racecourse at St. Petersburg,* by Dazario. © The Bridgeman Art Library.

p. 82   *The Flagellation of Christ,* by Adolphe-William Bouguereau (1825-1905), Cathedral of La Rochelle.

p. 84   *Philae, Egypt,* by David Roberts, (c. 1843) © The Fine Arts Society, London.

p. 88   *Couple in a Troika,* by Gustav Prucha (1875-1924). © The Bridgeman Art Library.

p. 91   The keyboard of the original organ presented by Handel to the Chapel of the Foundling Hospital, London. © The Bridgeman Art Library.

p. 95   *The Christmas Tree,* from the frontispiece of a musical by J. E. Carpenter and Henry Farmer. © The Bridgeman Art Library.

p. 96   *The Shepherdess,* by Adolphe-William Bouguereau (1825-1905), The Berkshire Museum, Pittsfield, Mass.

p.100   *Angels in a Heavenly Landscape,* by Benozzo di Lese di Sandro Gozzoli (1420-97), Palazzo-Medici-Riccardi, Florence.

p.103   Messiah, by George Frideric Handel, first edition covered in red leather with embossed gold decoration. © The Bridgeman Art Library.